HITTING HER W
TO THE NEGRO LEAGUES

A GRAPHIC NOVEL BIOGRAPHY OF
TONI STONE

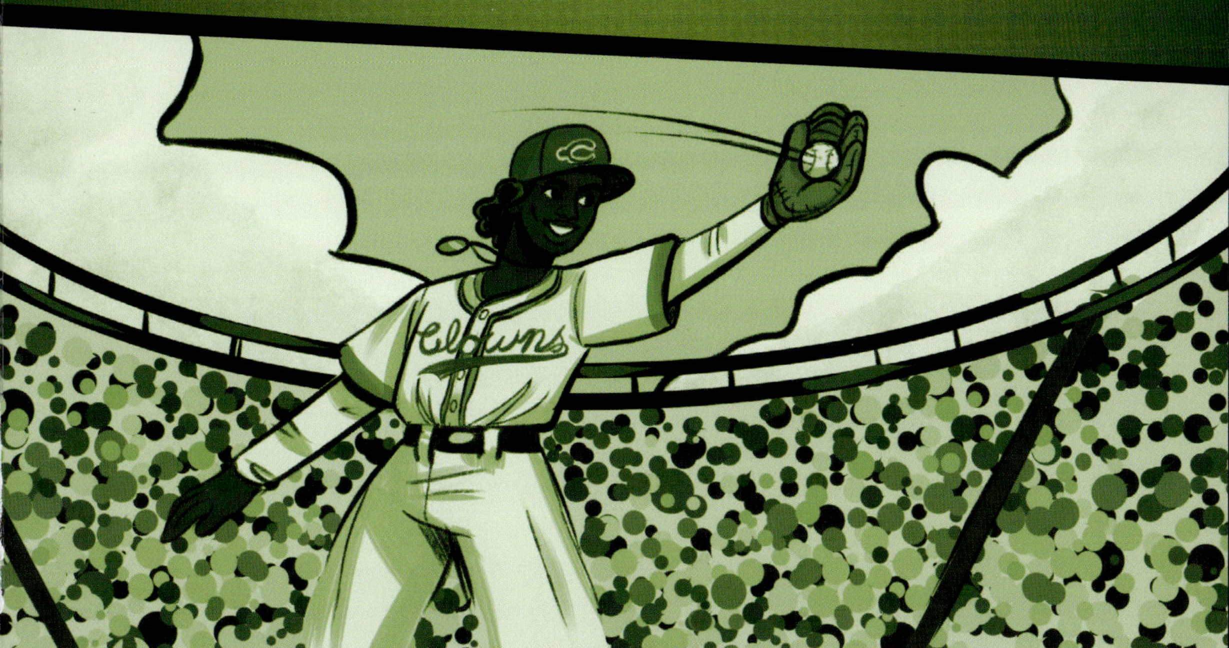
Clowns

WRITTEN BY MYRA FAYE TURNER ILLUSTRATED BY MARKIA JENAI

CAPSTONE PRESS
a capstone imprint

Published by Capstone Press, an imprint of Capstone
1710 Roe Crest Drive, North Mankato, Minnesota 56003
capstonepub.com

Copyright © 2025 by Capstone. All rights reserved. No part of this publication may be reproduced in whole or in part, or stored in a retrieval system, or transmitted in any form or by any means, electronic, mechanical, photocopying, recording, or otherwise, without written permission of the publisher.

Library of Congress Cataloging-in-Publication Data is available on the Library of Congress website.
ISBN: 9781669083245 (hardcover)
ISBN: 9781669083191 (paperback)
ISBN: 9781669083207 (eBook PDF)

Summary: In the early 1950s, Toni Stone made history as the first Black woman to play professional baseball. In this action-packed graphic novel, discover Stone's journey from a young "tomboy" in Saint Paul, Minnesota, to a starting second baseman with the Negro American League's Indianapolis Clowns. Despite racial and gender barriers, this groundbreaking ballplayer achieved success on the field—like getting a rare hit off baseball legend Satchel Paige—and inspired countless young women off the field.

Editorial Credits
Editor: Donald Lemke; Designer: Bobbie Nuytten; Production Specialist: Whitney Schaefer

Image Credit
Getty Images: Transcendental Graphics, 28

Any additional websites and resources referenced in this book are not maintained, authorized, or sponsored by Capstone. All product and company names are trademark™ or registered trademarks® of their respective holders.

TABLE OF CONTENTS

Tomboy Stone 4
The Minnesota Kid 6
Barnstorming 10
Ms. Toni Stone 16
End of an Era 22

    More About Toni Stone and the
        Negro Leagues 28
    Glossary 30
    Read More 31
    Internet Sites 31
    About the Author 32
    About the Illustrator 32

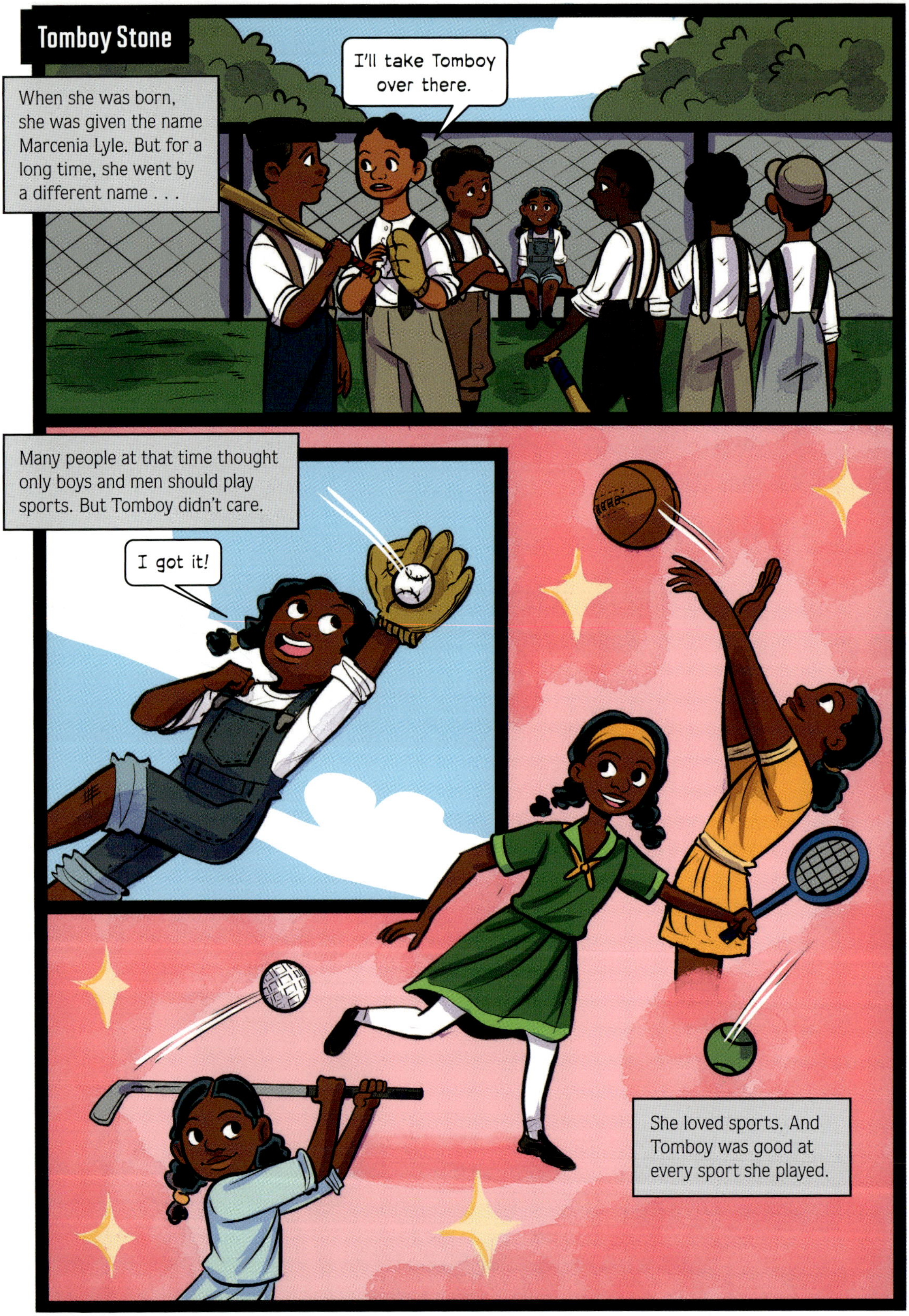
Tomboy Stone
When she was born, she was given the name Marcenia Lyle. But for a long time, she went by a different name . . .
I'll take Tomboy over there.
Many people at that time thought only boys and men should play sports. But Tomboy didn't care.
I got it!
She loved sports. And Tomboy was good at every sport she played.

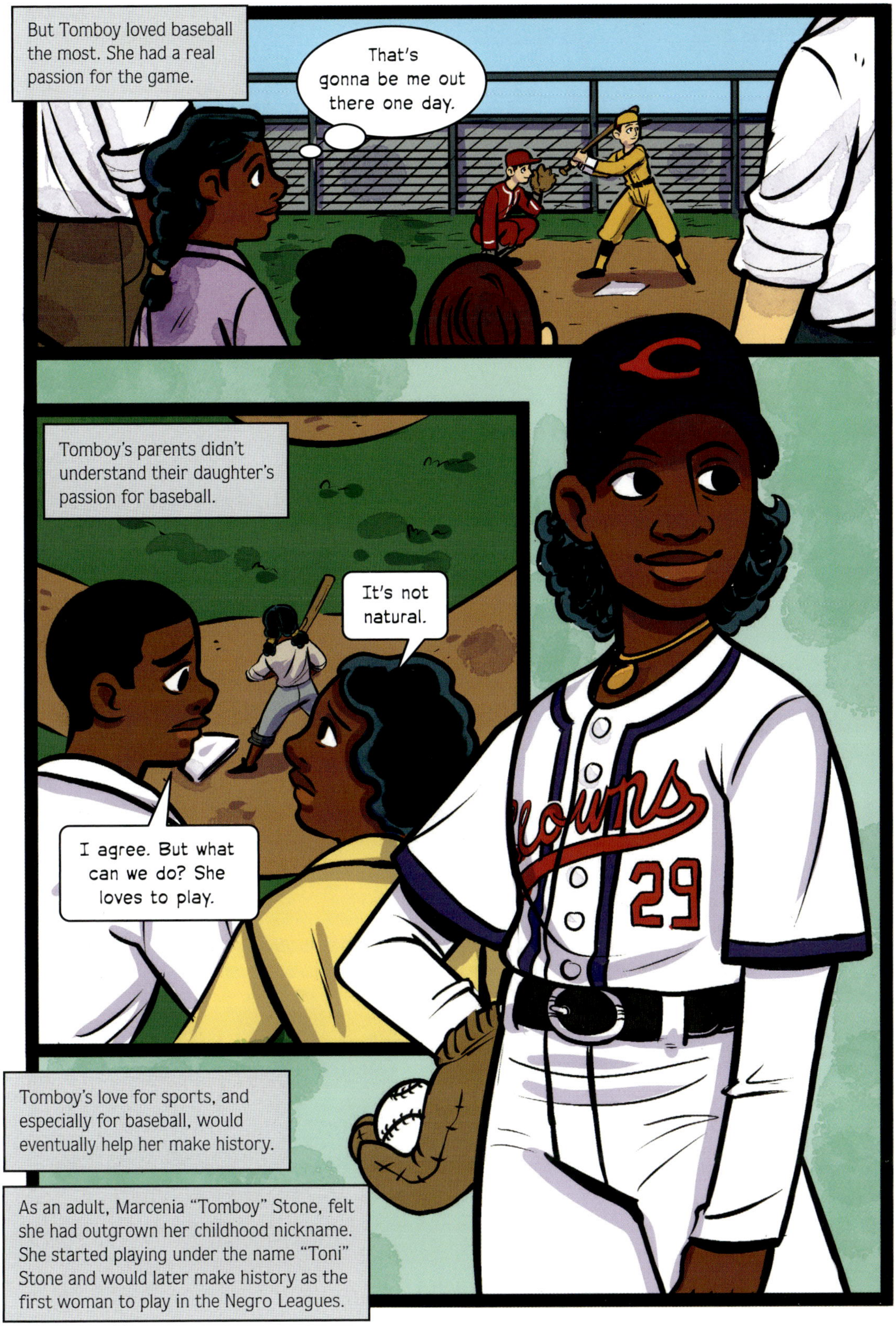
But Tomboy loved baseball the most. She had a real passion for the game.
That's gonna be me out there one day.
Tomboy's parents didn't understand their daughter's passion for baseball.
It's not natural.
I agree. But what can we do? She loves to play.
Clowns
29
Tomboy's love for sports, and especially for baseball, would eventually help her make history.
As an adult, Marcenia "Tomboy" Stone, felt she had outgrown her childhood nickname. She started playing under the name "Toni" Stone and would later make history as the first woman to play in the Negro Leagues.

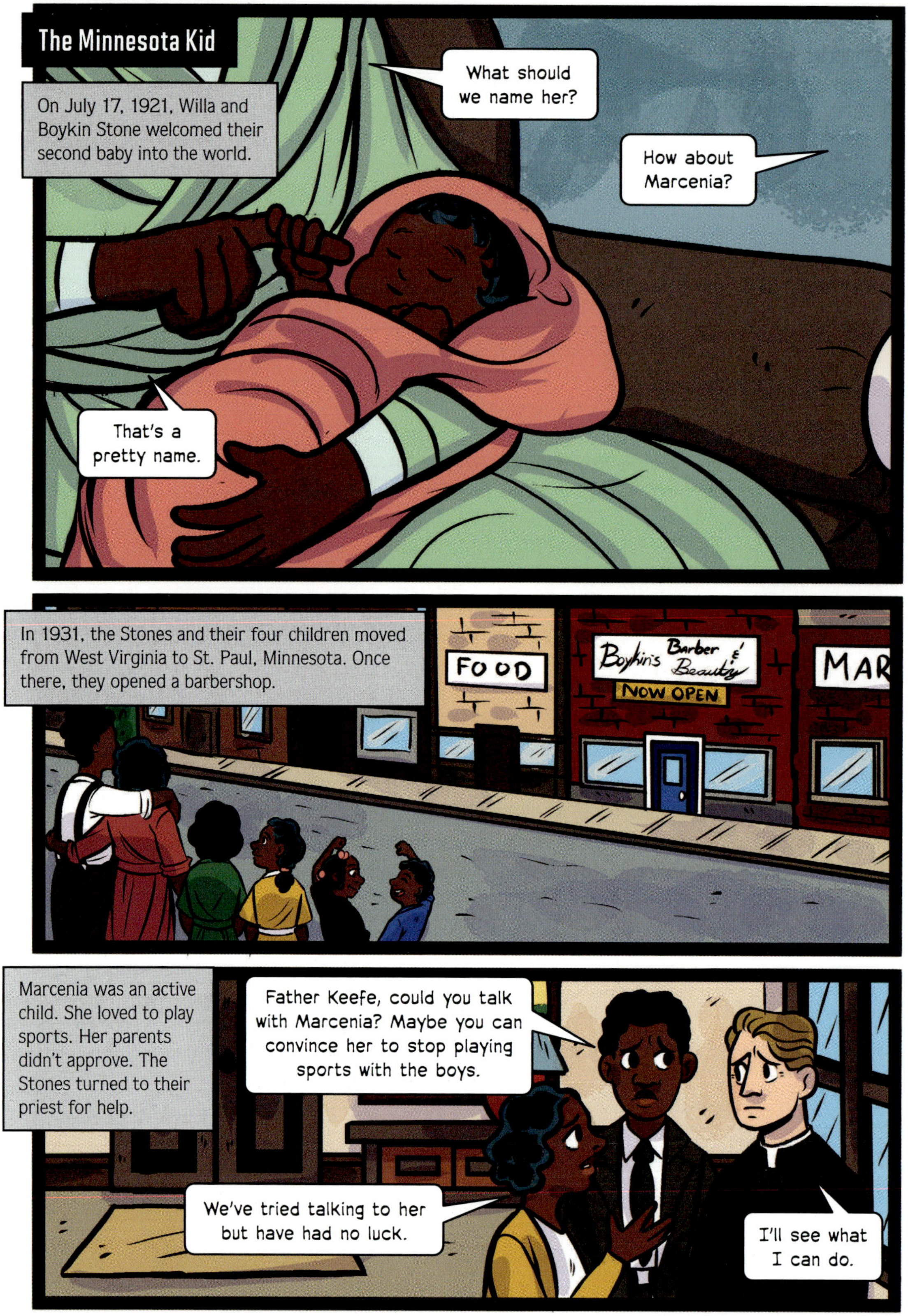
The Minnesota Kid
On July 17, 1921, Willa and Boykin Stone welcomed their second baby into the world.
What should we name her?
How about Marcenia?
That's a pretty name.
In 1931, the Stones and their four children moved from West Virginia to St. Paul, Minnesota. Once there, they opened a barbershop.
FOOD
Boykin's Barber & Beauty
NOW OPEN
MAR
Marcenia was an active child. She loved to play sports. Her parents didn't approve. The Stones turned to their priest for help.
Father Keefe, could you talk with Marcenia? Maybe you can convince her to stop playing sports with the boys.
We've tried talking to her but have had no luck.
I'll see what I can do.

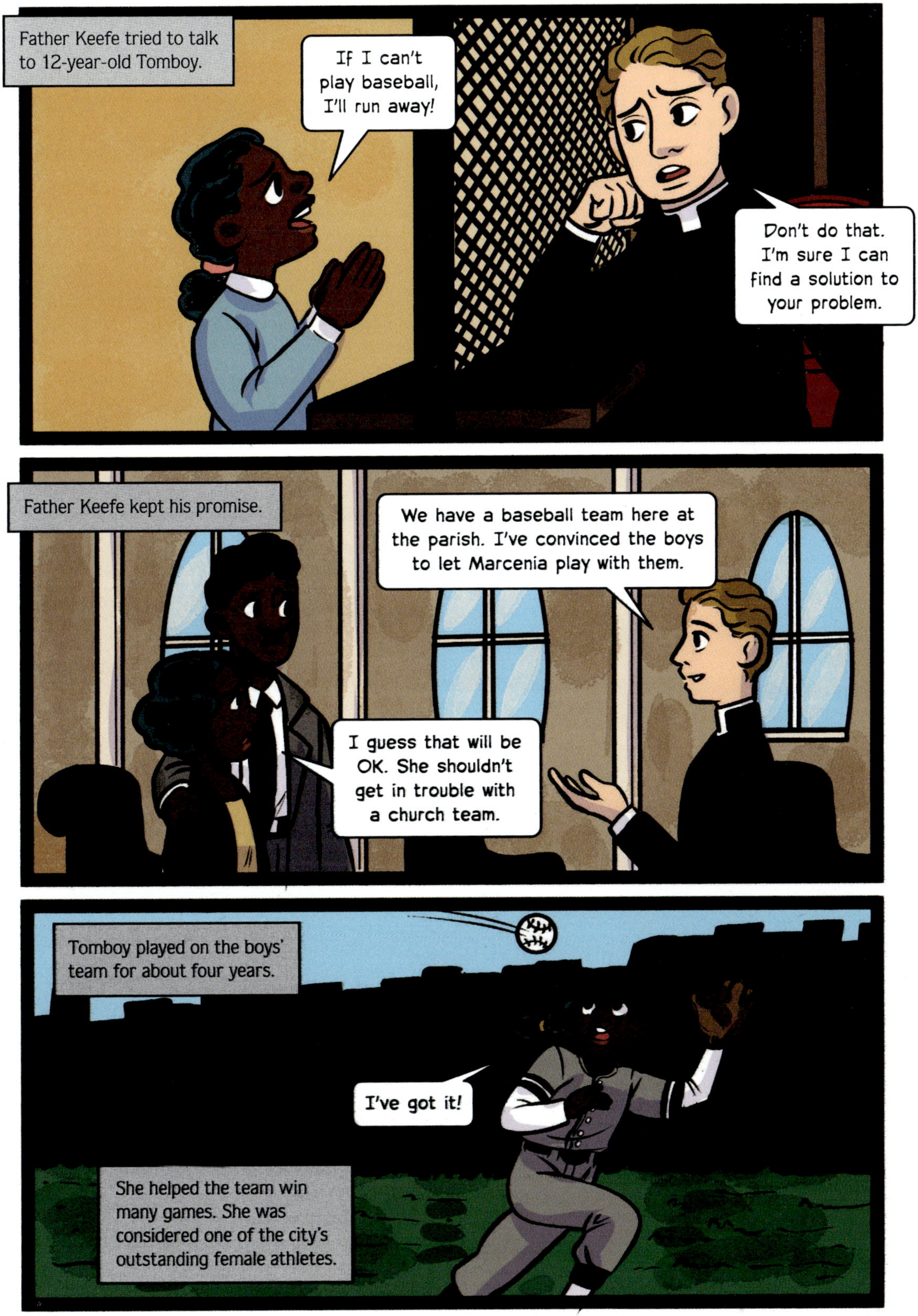
Father Keefe tried to talk to 12-year-old Tomboy.
If I can't play baseball, I'll run away!
Don't do that. I'm sure I can find a solution to your problem.
Father Keefe kept his promise.
We have a baseball team here at the parish. I've convinced the boys to let Marcenia play with them.
I guess that will be OK. She shouldn't get in trouble with a church team.
Tomboy played on the boys' team for about four years.
I've got it!
She helped the team win many games. She was considered one of the city's outstanding female athletes.

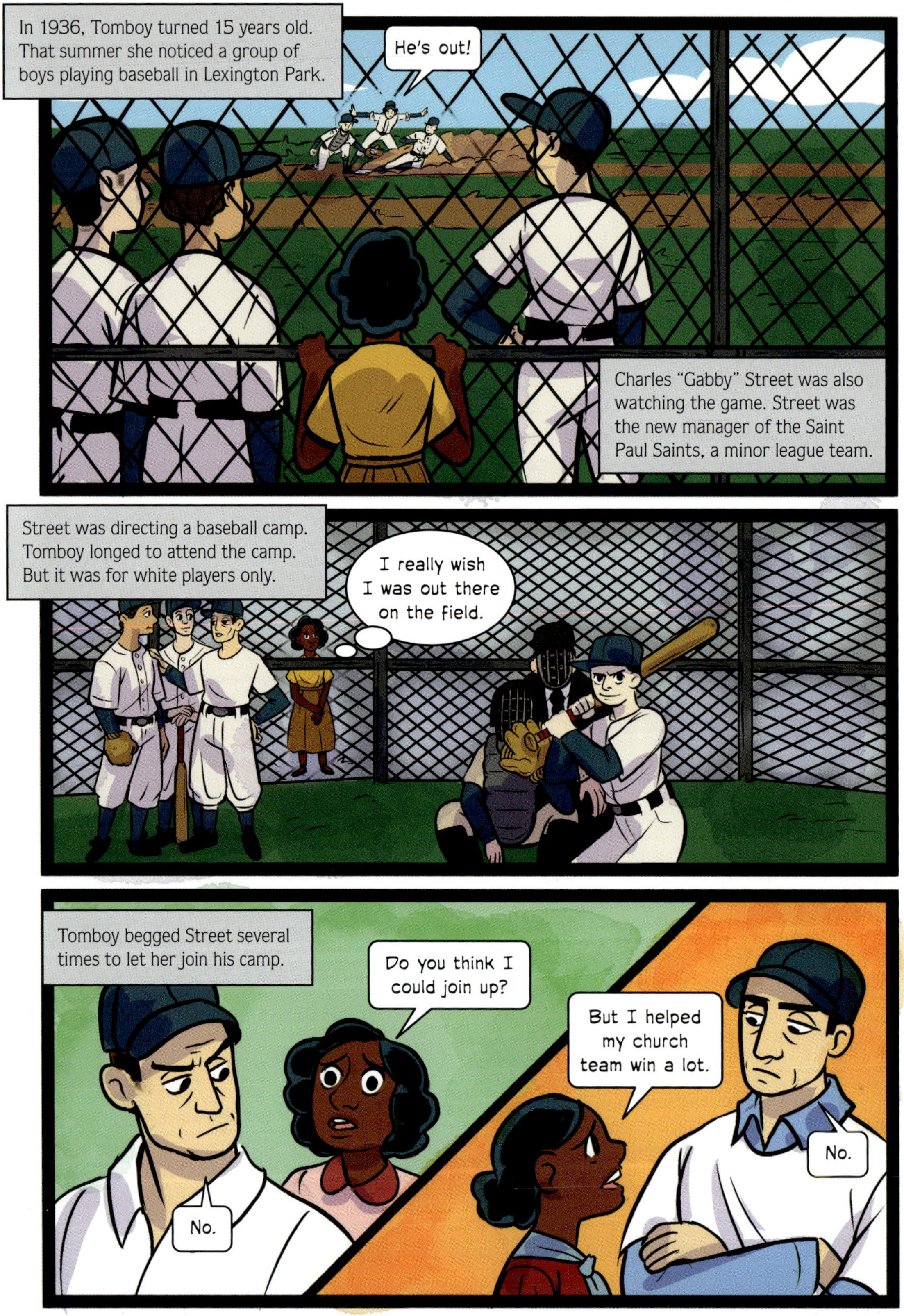
In 1936, Tomboy turned 15 years old. That summer she noticed a group of boys playing baseball in Lexington Park.
He's out!
Charles "Gabby" Street was also watching the game. Street was the new manager of the Saint Paul Saints, a minor league team.
Street was directing a baseball camp. Tomboy longed to attend the camp. But it was for white players only.
I really wish I was out there on the field.
Tomboy begged Street several times to let her join his camp.
Do you think I could join up?
No.
But I helped my church team win a lot.
No.

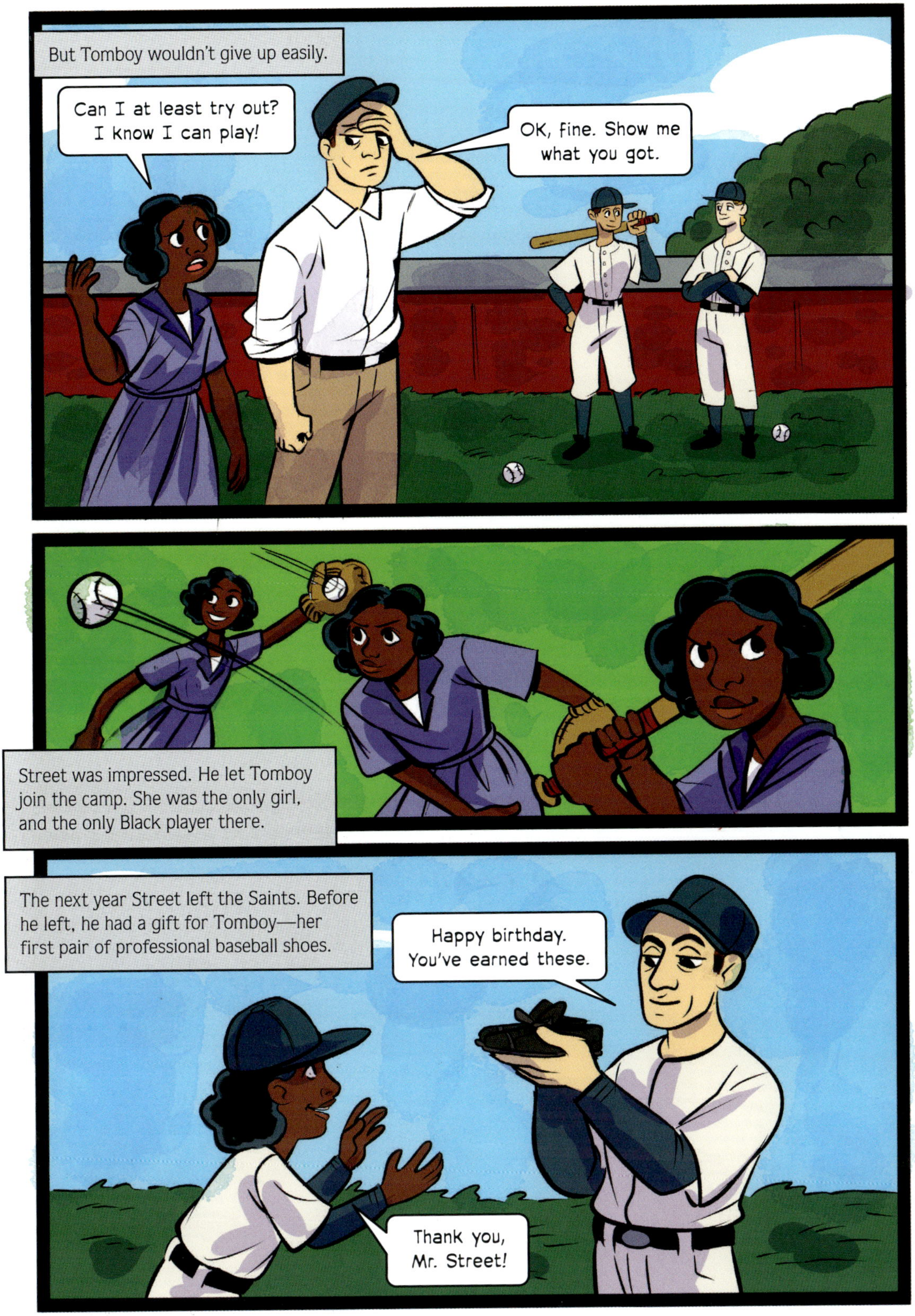
But Tomboy wouldn't give up easily.
Can I at least try out? I know I can play!
OK, fine. Show me what you got.
Street was impressed. He let Tomboy join the camp. She was the only girl, and the only Black player there.
The next year Street left the Saints. Before he left, he had a gift for Tomboy—her first pair of professional baseball shoes.
Happy birthday. You've earned these.
Thank you, Mr. Street!

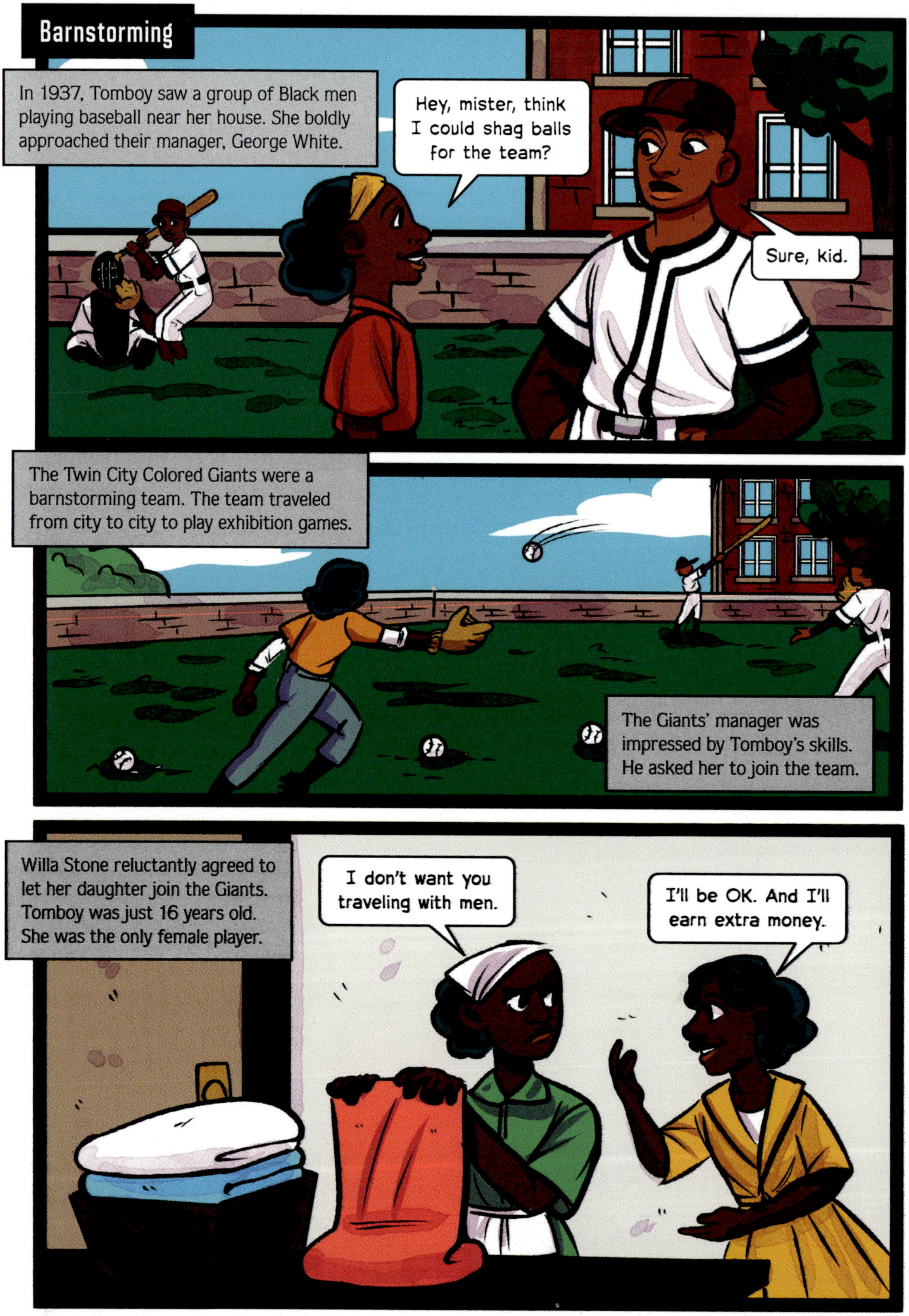
Barnstorming
In 1937, Tomboy saw a group of Black men playing baseball near her house. She boldly approached their manager, George White.
Hey, mister, think I could shag balls for the team?
Sure, kid.
The Twin City Colored Giants were a barnstorming team. The team traveled from city to city to play exhibition games.
The Giants' manager was impressed by Tomboy's skills. He asked her to join the team.
Willa Stone reluctantly agreed to let her daughter join the Giants. Tomboy was just 16 years old. She was the only female player.
I don't want you traveling with men.
I'll be OK. And I'll earn extra money.

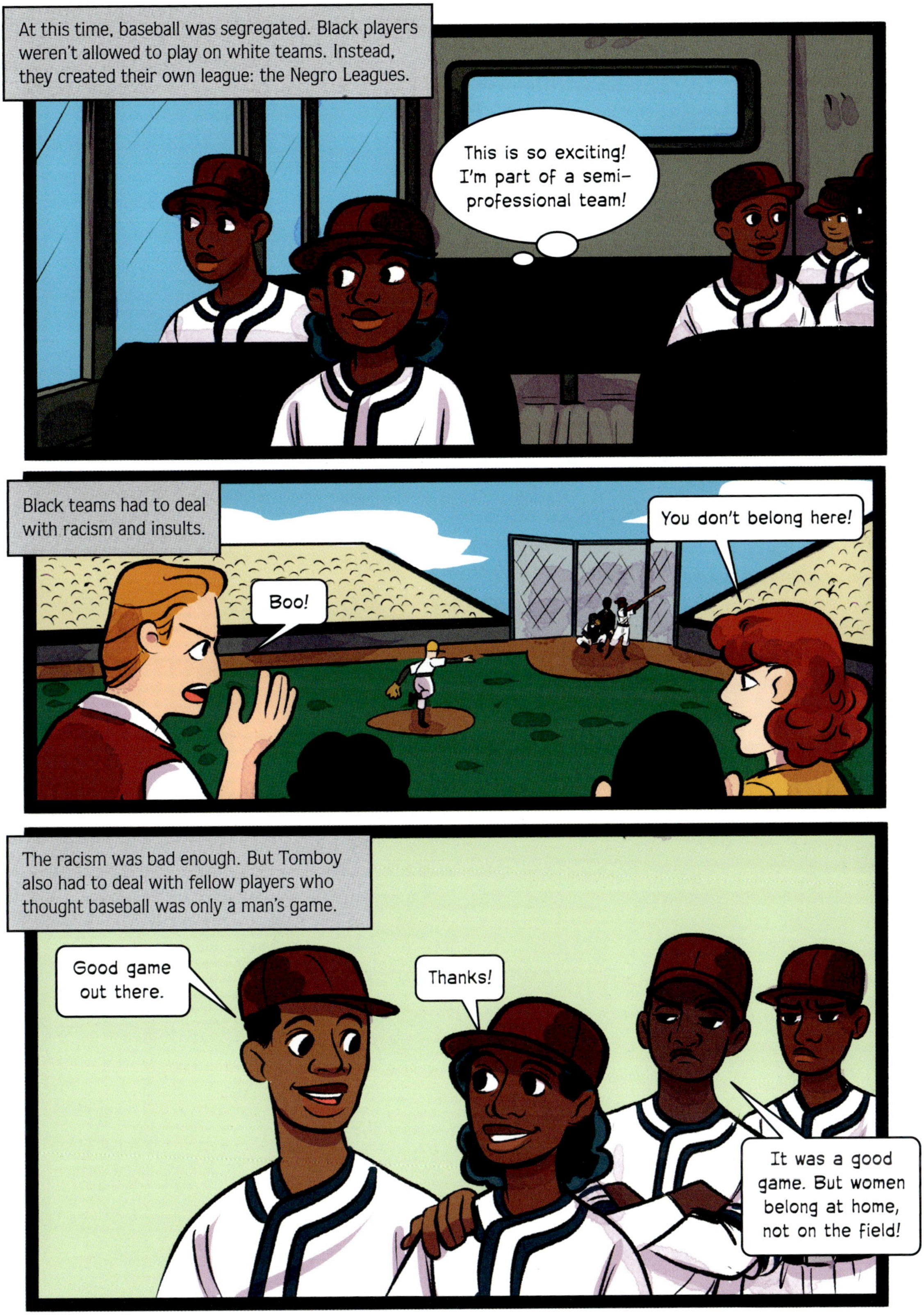
At this time, baseball was segregated. Black players weren't allowed to play on white teams. Instead, they created their own league: the Negro Leagues.
This is so exciting! I'm part of a semi-professional team!
Black teams had to deal with racism and insults.
Boo!
You don't belong here!
The racism was bad enough. But Tomboy also had to deal with fellow players who thought baseball was only a man's game.
Good game out there.
Thanks!
It was a good game. But women belong at home, not on the field!

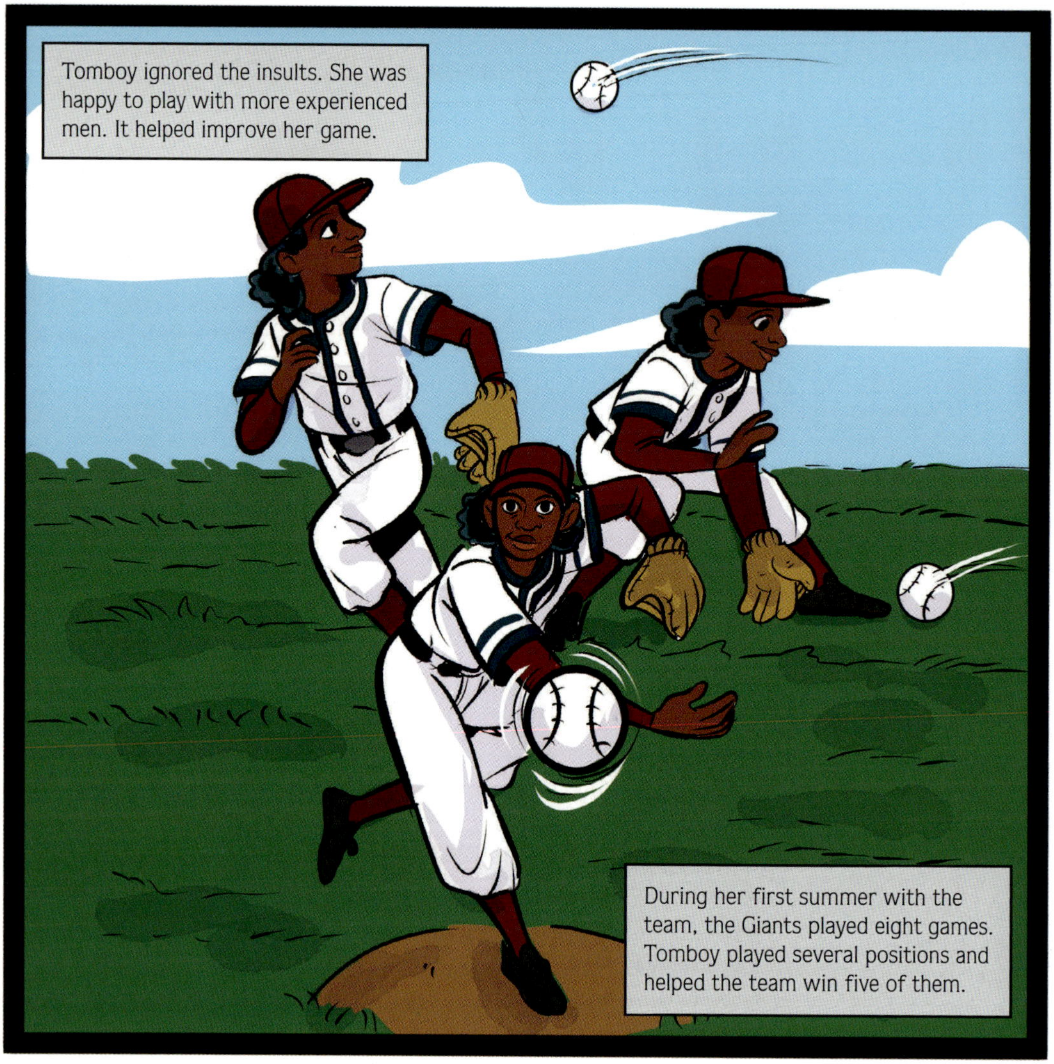
Tomboy ignored the insults. She was happy to play with more experienced men. It helped improve her game.
During her first summer with the team, the Giants played eight games. Tomboy played several positions and helped the team win five of them.

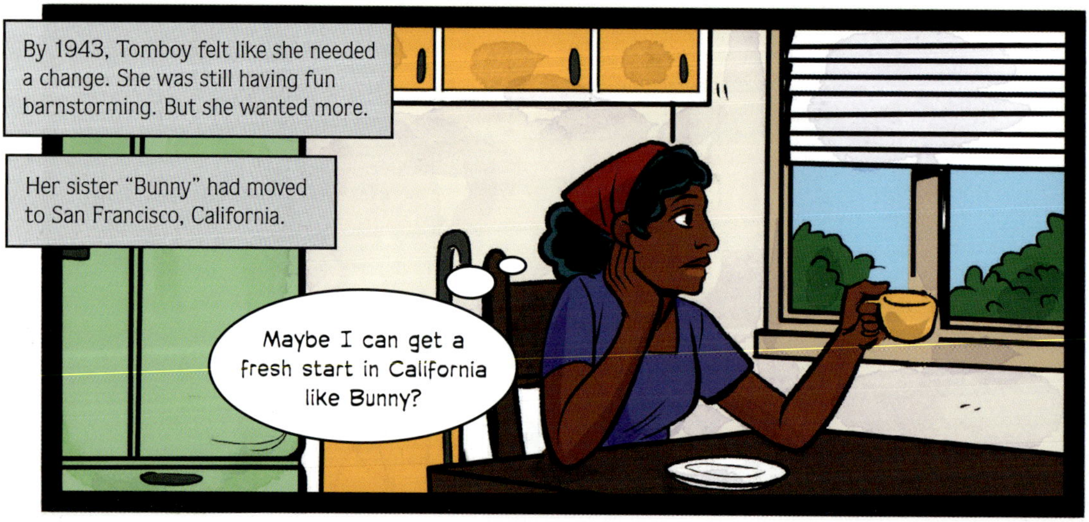
By 1943, Tomboy felt like she needed a change. She was still having fun barnstorming. But she wanted more.
Her sister "Bunny" had moved to San Francisco, California.
Maybe I can get a fresh start in California like Bunny?

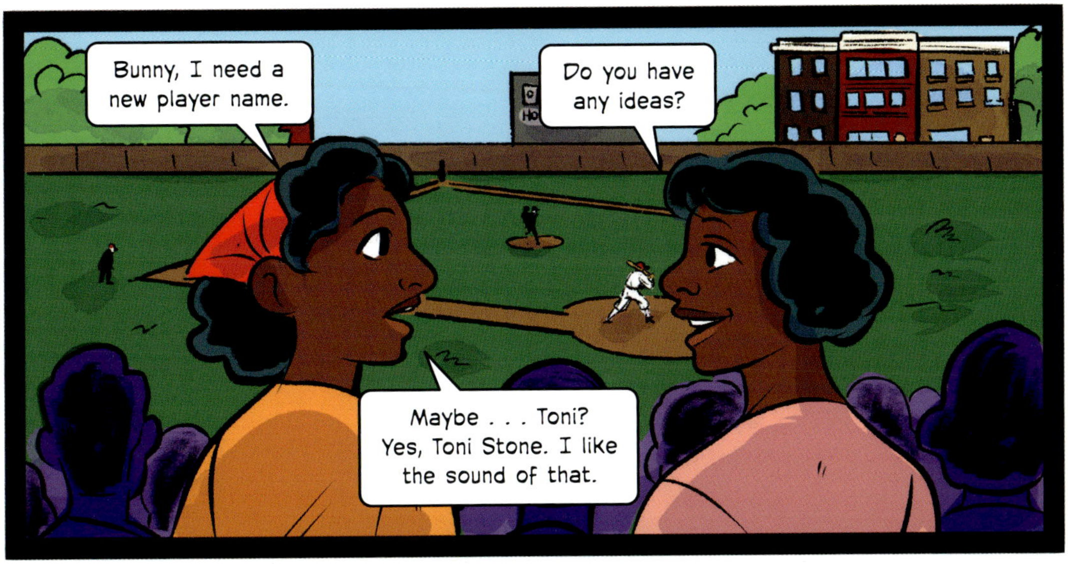

Bunny, I need a new player name.
Do you have any ideas?
Maybe . . . Toni? Yes, Toni Stone. I like the sound of that.

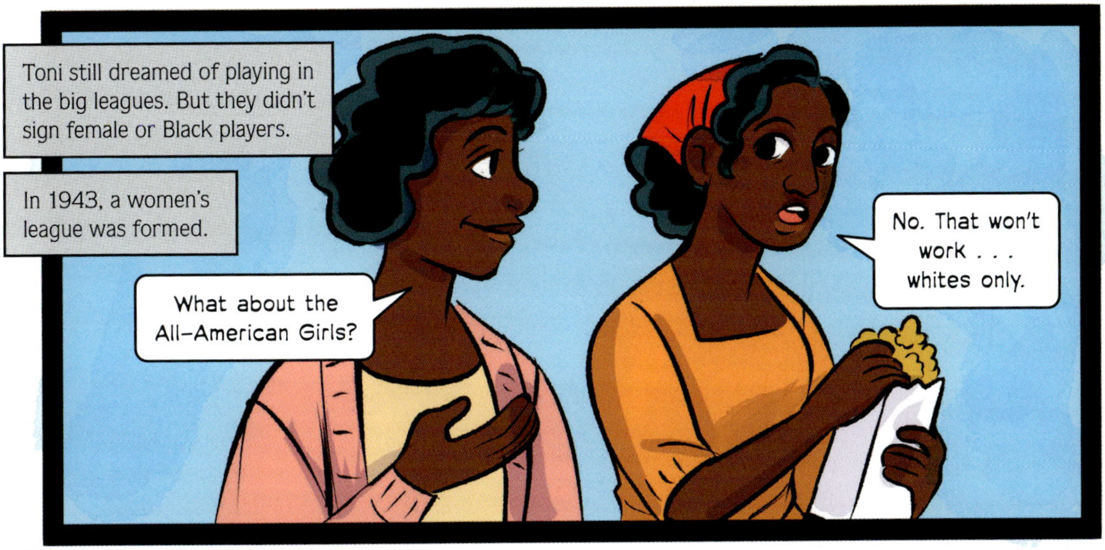

Toni still dreamed of playing in the big leagues. But they didn't sign female or Black players.
In 1943, a women's league was formed.
What about the All-American Girls?
No. That won't work . . . whites only.

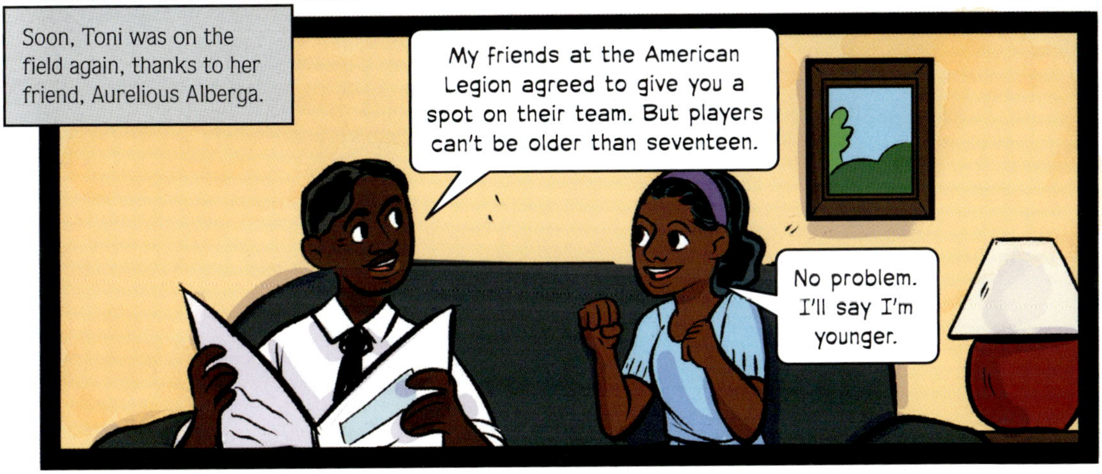

Soon, Toni was on the field again, thanks to her friend, Aurelious Alberga.
My friends at the American Legion agreed to give you a spot on their team. But players can't be older than seventeen.
No problem. I'll say I'm younger.

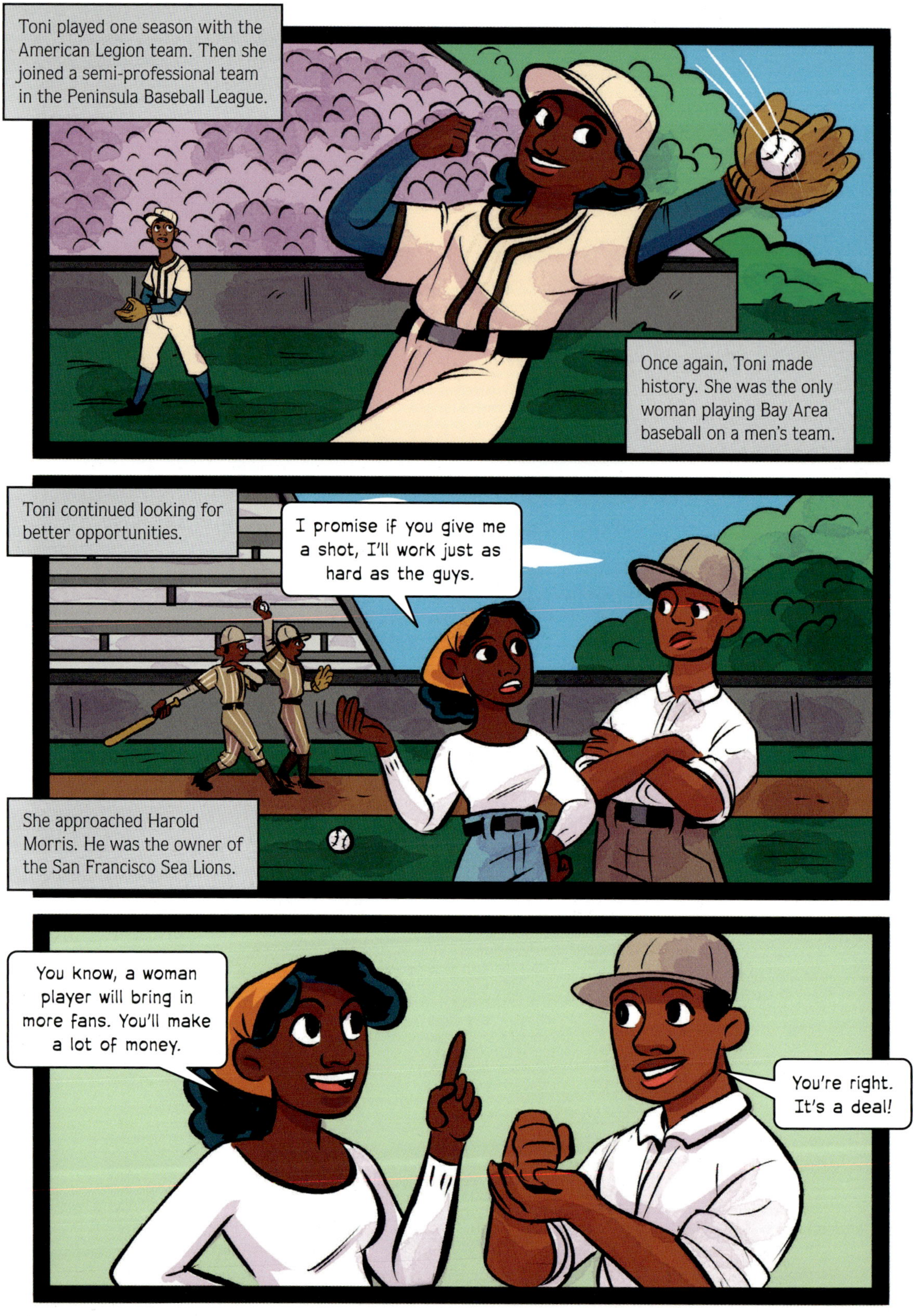
Toni played one season with the American Legion team. Then she joined a semi-professional team in the Peninsula Baseball League.
Once again, Toni made history. She was the only woman playing Bay Area baseball on a men's team.
Toni continued looking for better opportunities.
I promise if you give me a shot, I'll work just as hard as the guys.
She approached Harold Morris. He was the owner of the San Francisco Sea Lions.
You know, a woman player will bring in more fans. You'll make a lot of money.
You're right. It's a deal!

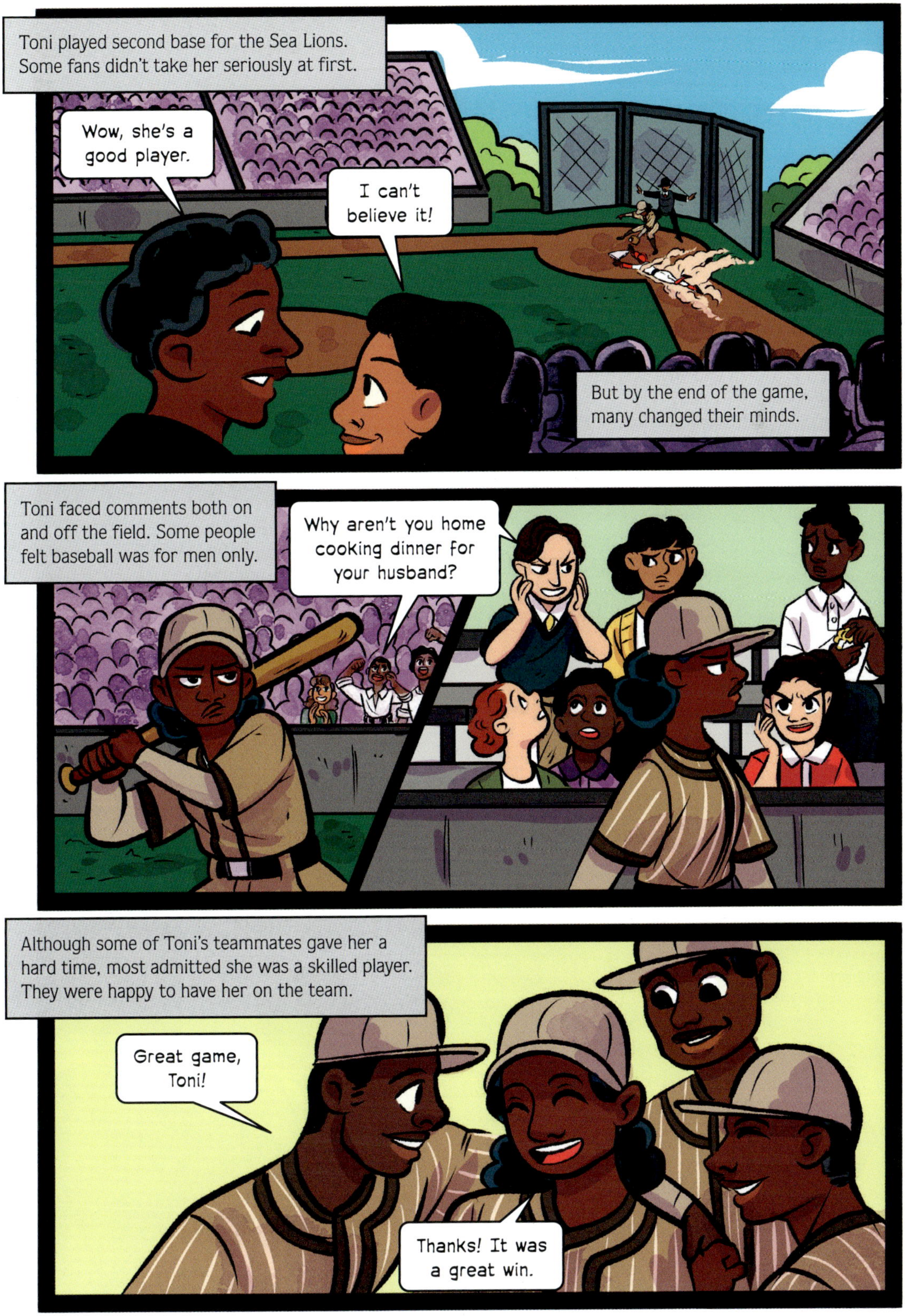
Toni played second base for the Sea Lions. Some fans didn't take her seriously at first.
Wow, she's a good player.
I can't believe it!
But by the end of the game, many changed their minds.
Toni faced comments both on and off the field. Some people felt baseball was for men only.
Why aren't you home cooking dinner for your husband?
Although some of Toni's teammates gave her a hard time, most admitted she was a skilled player. They were happy to have her on the team.
Great game, Toni!
Thanks! It was a great win.

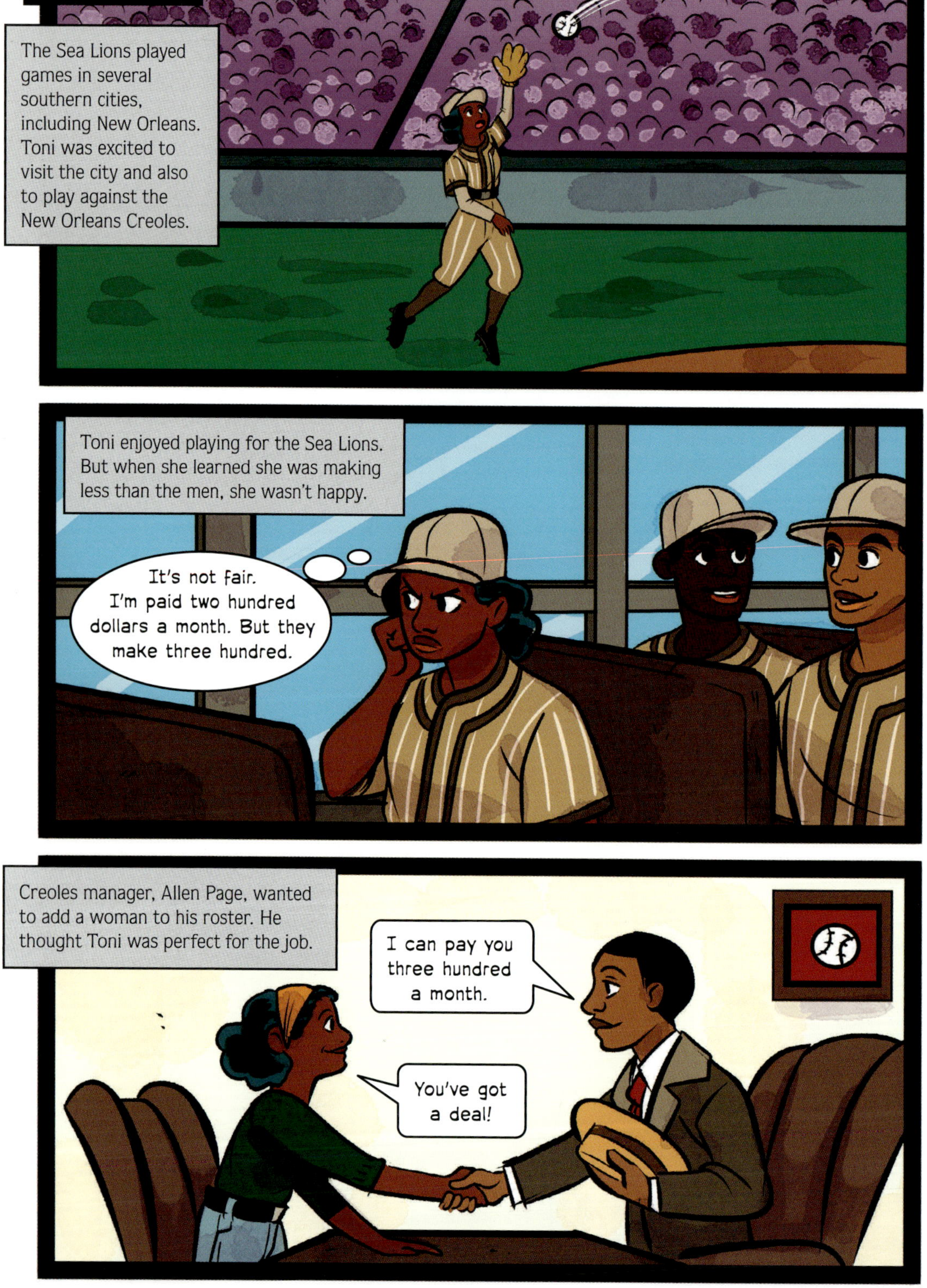
The Sea Lions played games in several southern cities, including New Orleans. Toni was excited to visit the city and also to play against the New Orleans Creoles.
Toni enjoyed playing for the Sea Lions. But when she learned she was making less than the men, she wasn't happy.
It's not fair. I'm paid two hundred dollars a month. But they make three hundred.
Creoles manager, Allen Page, wanted to add a woman to his roster. He thought Toni was perfect for the job.
I can pay you three hundred a month.
You've got a deal!

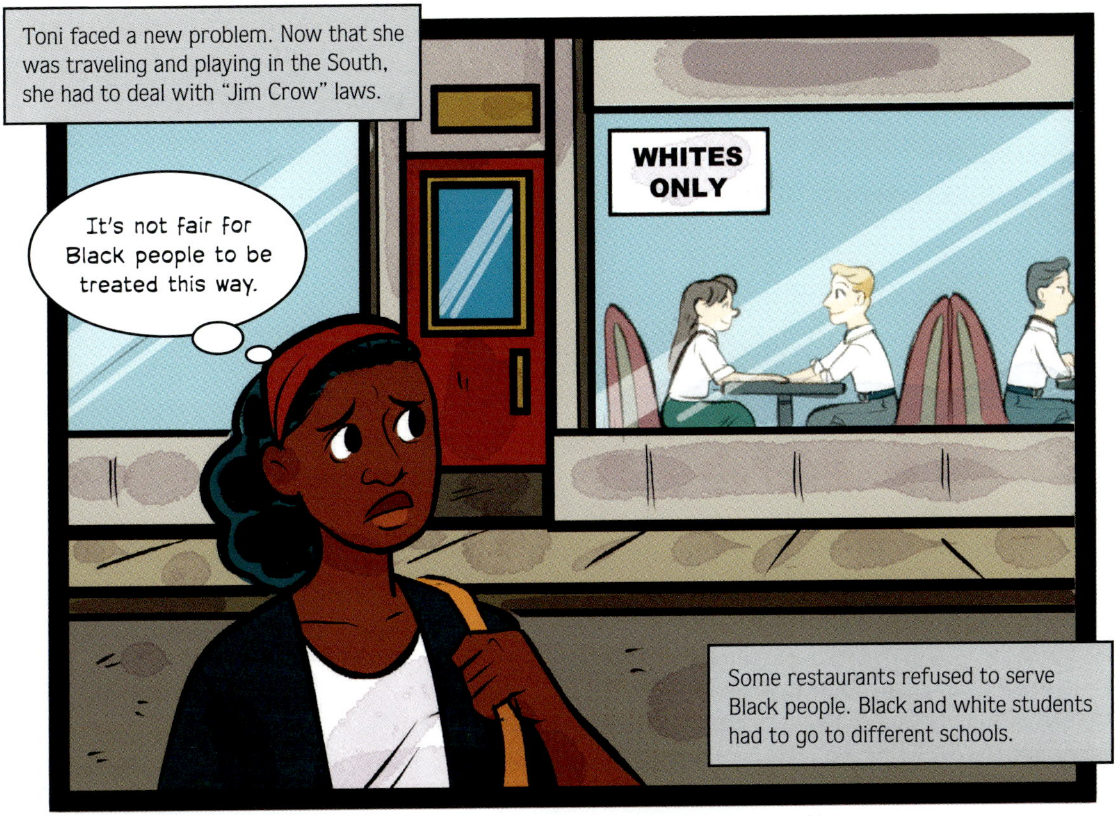
Toni faced a new problem. Now that she was traveling and playing in the South, she had to deal with "Jim Crow" laws.
WHITES ONLY
It's not fair for Black people to be treated this way.
Some restaurants refused to serve Black people. Black and white students had to go to different schools.

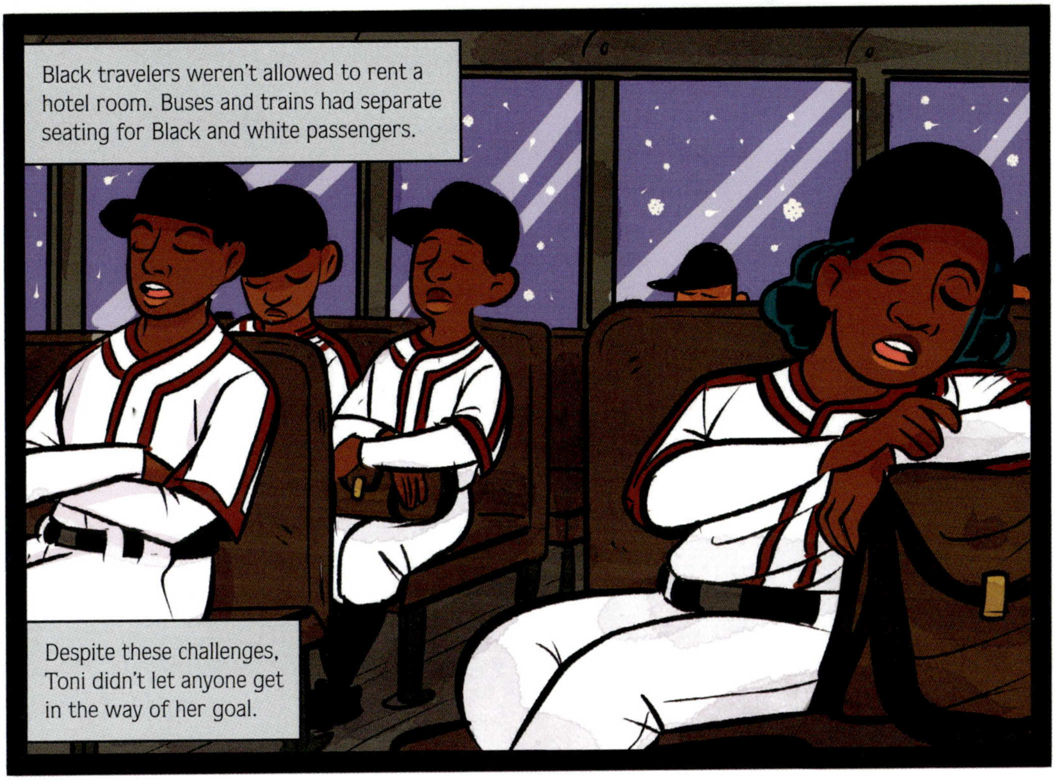
Black travelers weren't allowed to rent a hotel room. Buses and trains had separate seating for Black and white passengers.
Despite these challenges, Toni didn't let anyone get in the way of her goal.

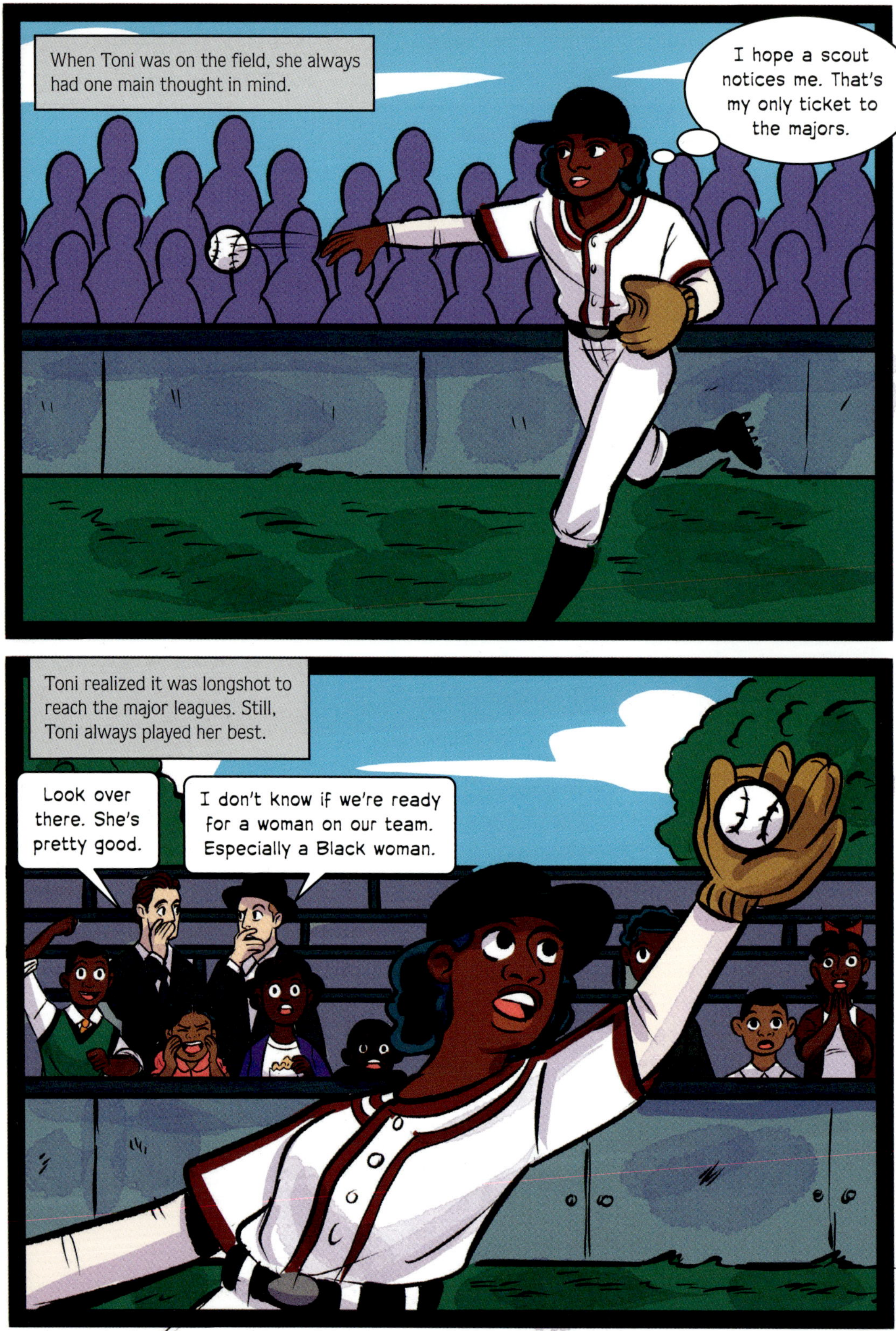
When Toni was on the field, she always had one main thought in mind.
I hope a scout notices me. That's my only ticket to the majors.
Toni realized it was longshot to reach the major leagues. Still, Toni always played her best.
Look over there. She's pretty good.
I don't know if we're ready for a woman on our team. Especially a Black woman.

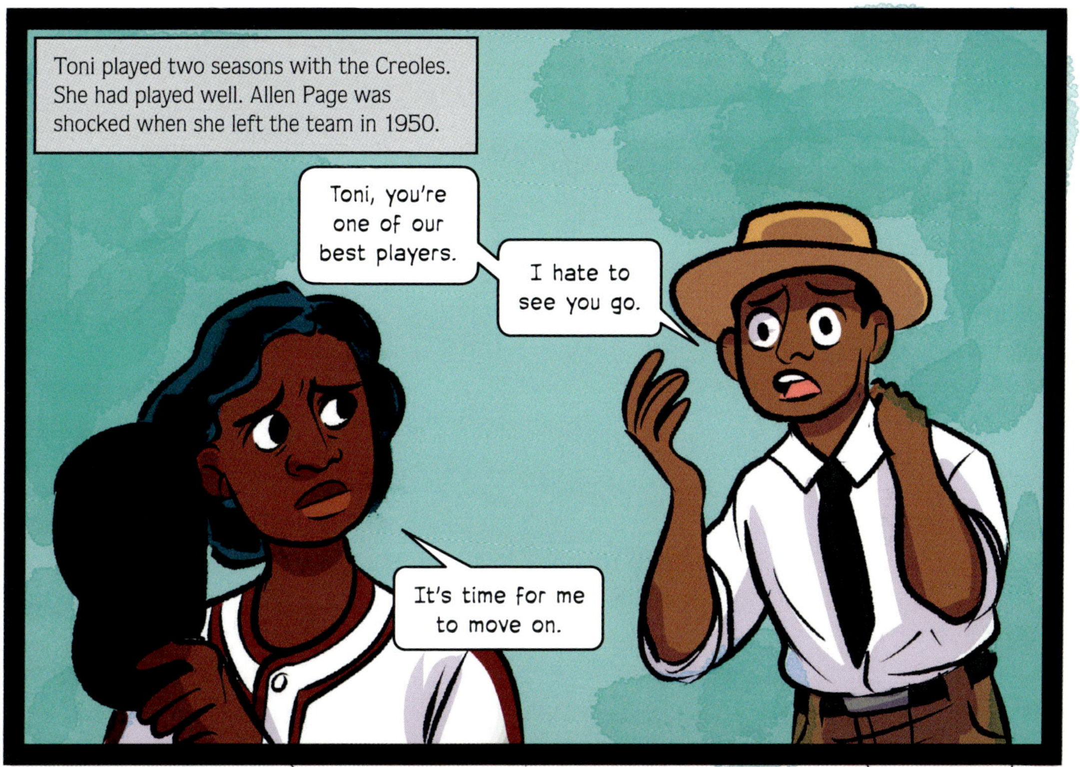
Toni played two seasons with the Creoles. She had played well. Allen Page was shocked when she left the team in 1950.
Toni, you're one of our best players.
I hate to see you go.
It's time for me to move on.

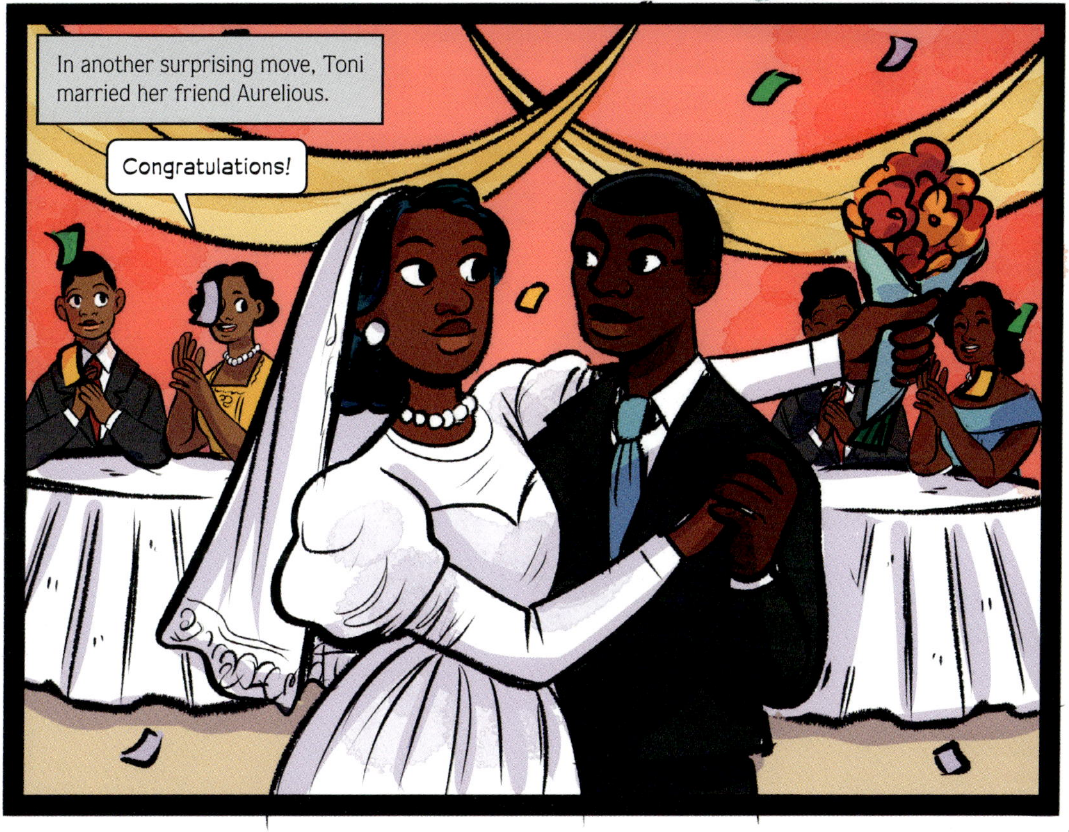
In another surprising move, Toni married her friend Aurelious.
Congratulations!

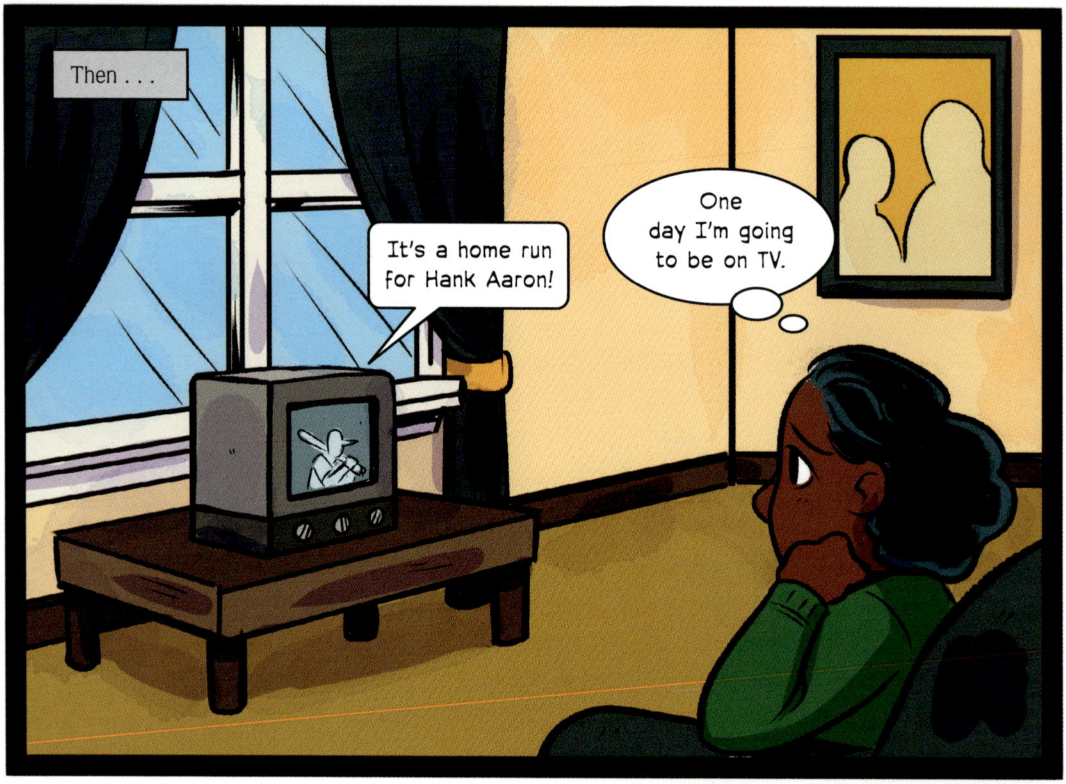
Then . . .
It's a home run for Hank Aaron!
One day I'm going to be on TV.

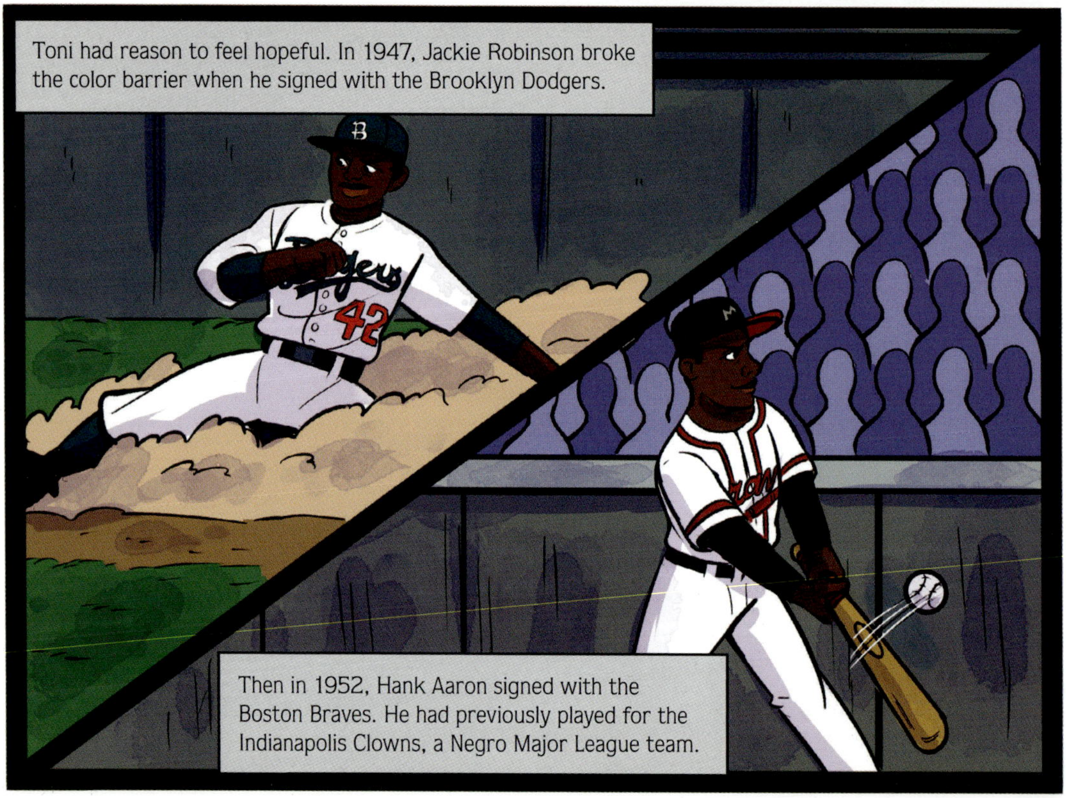
Toni had reason to feel hopeful. In 1947, Jackie Robinson broke the color barrier when he signed with the Brooklyn Dodgers.
Then in 1952, Hank Aaron signed with the Boston Braves. He had previously played for the Indianapolis Clowns, a Negro Major League team.

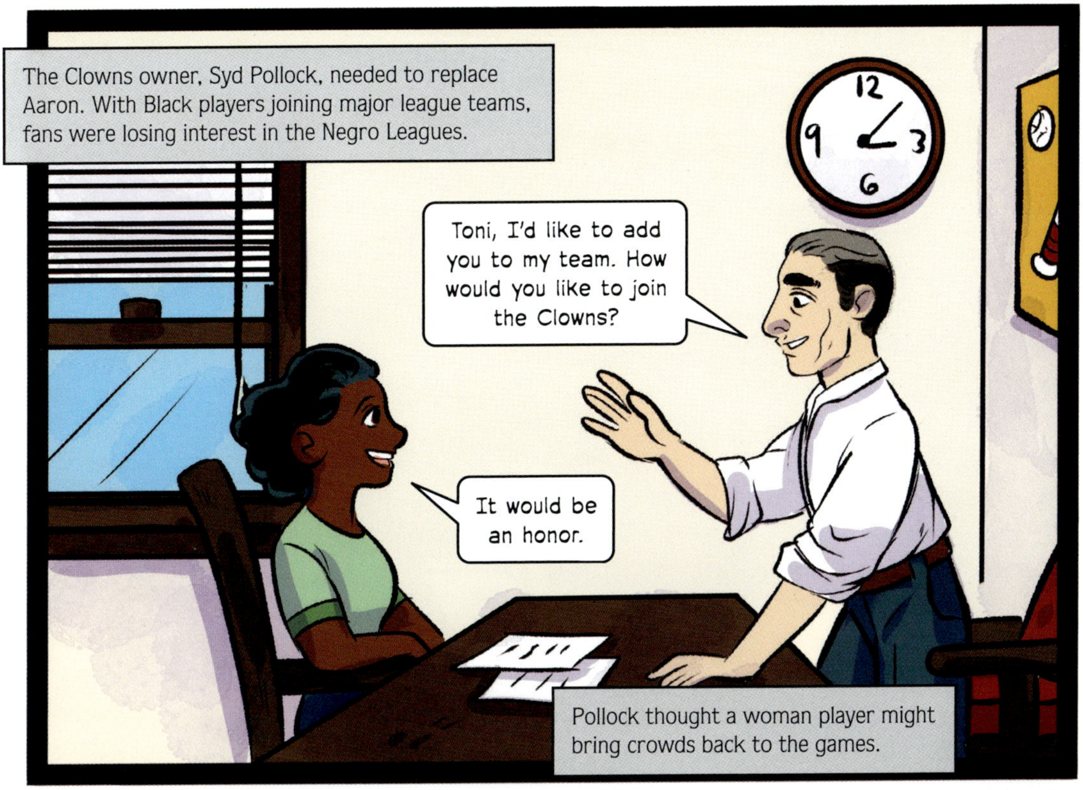
The Clowns owner, Syd Pollock, needed to replace Aaron. With Black players joining major league teams, fans were losing interest in the Negro Leagues.
Toni, I'd like to add you to my team. How would you like to join the Clowns?
It would be an honor.
Pollock thought a woman player might bring crowds back to the games.

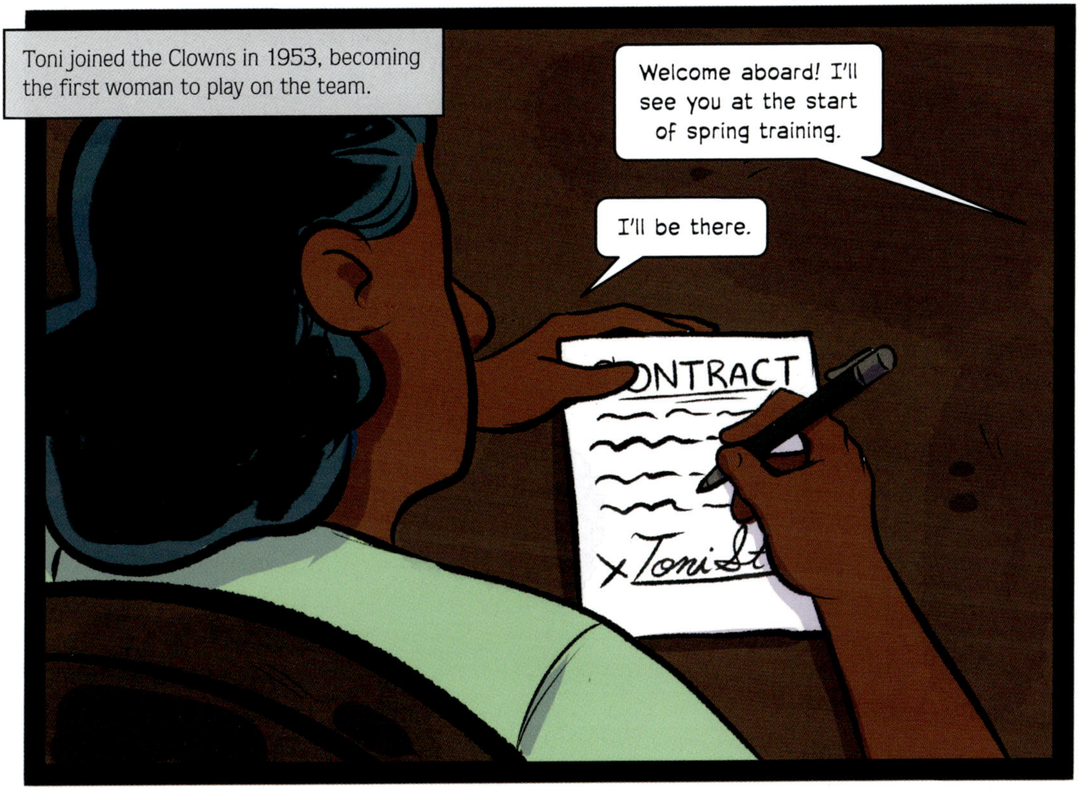
Toni joined the Clowns in 1953, becoming the first woman to play on the team.
Welcome aboard! I'll see you at the start of spring training.
I'll be there.

End of an Era

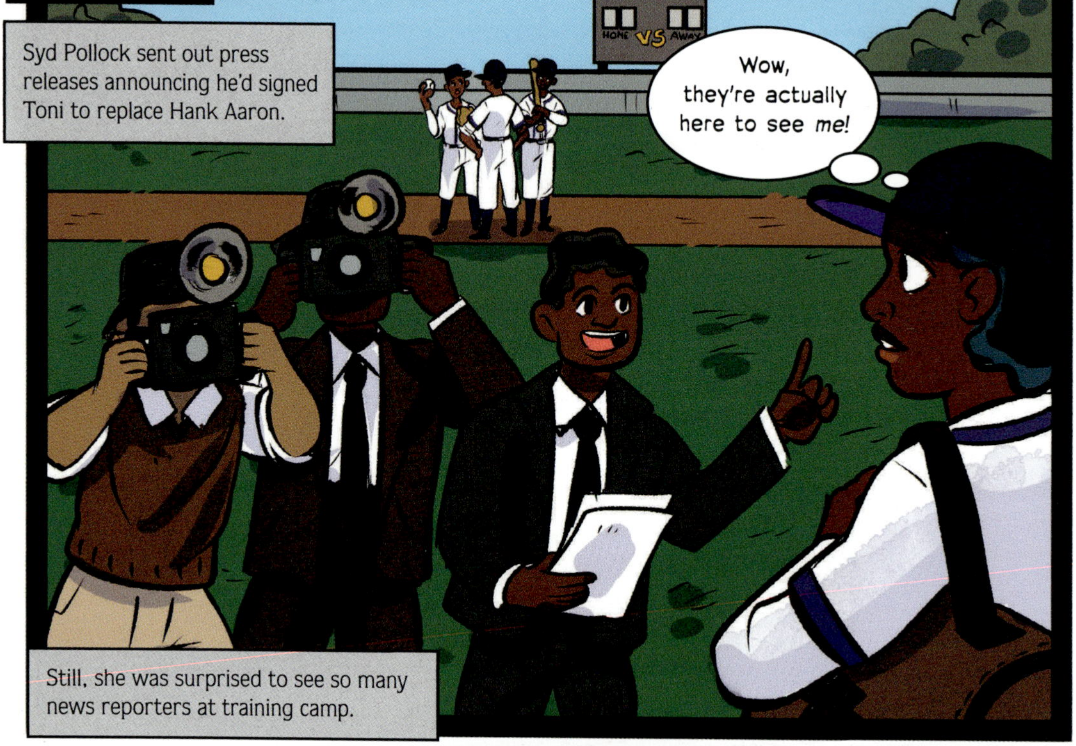
Syd Pollock sent out press releases announcing he'd signed Toni to replace Hank Aaron.
HOME VS AWAY
Wow, they're actually here to see *me!*
Still, she was surprised to see so many news reporters at training camp.

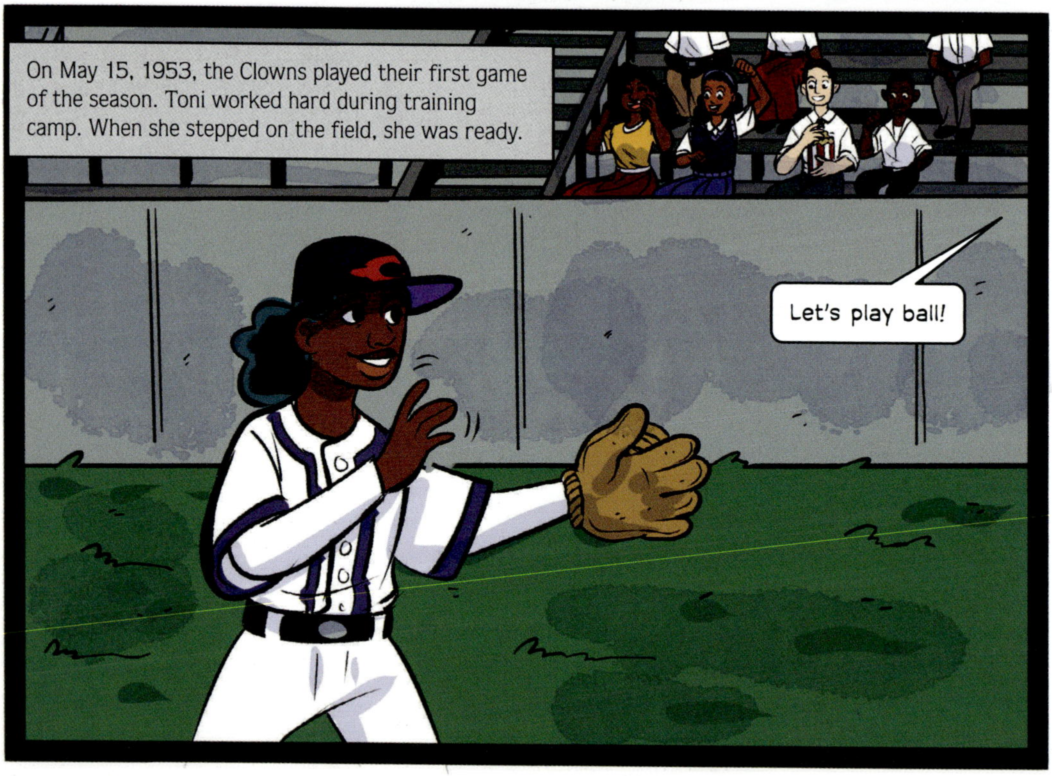
On May 15, 1953, the Clowns played their first game of the season. Toni worked hard during training camp. When she stepped on the field, she was ready.
Let's play ball!

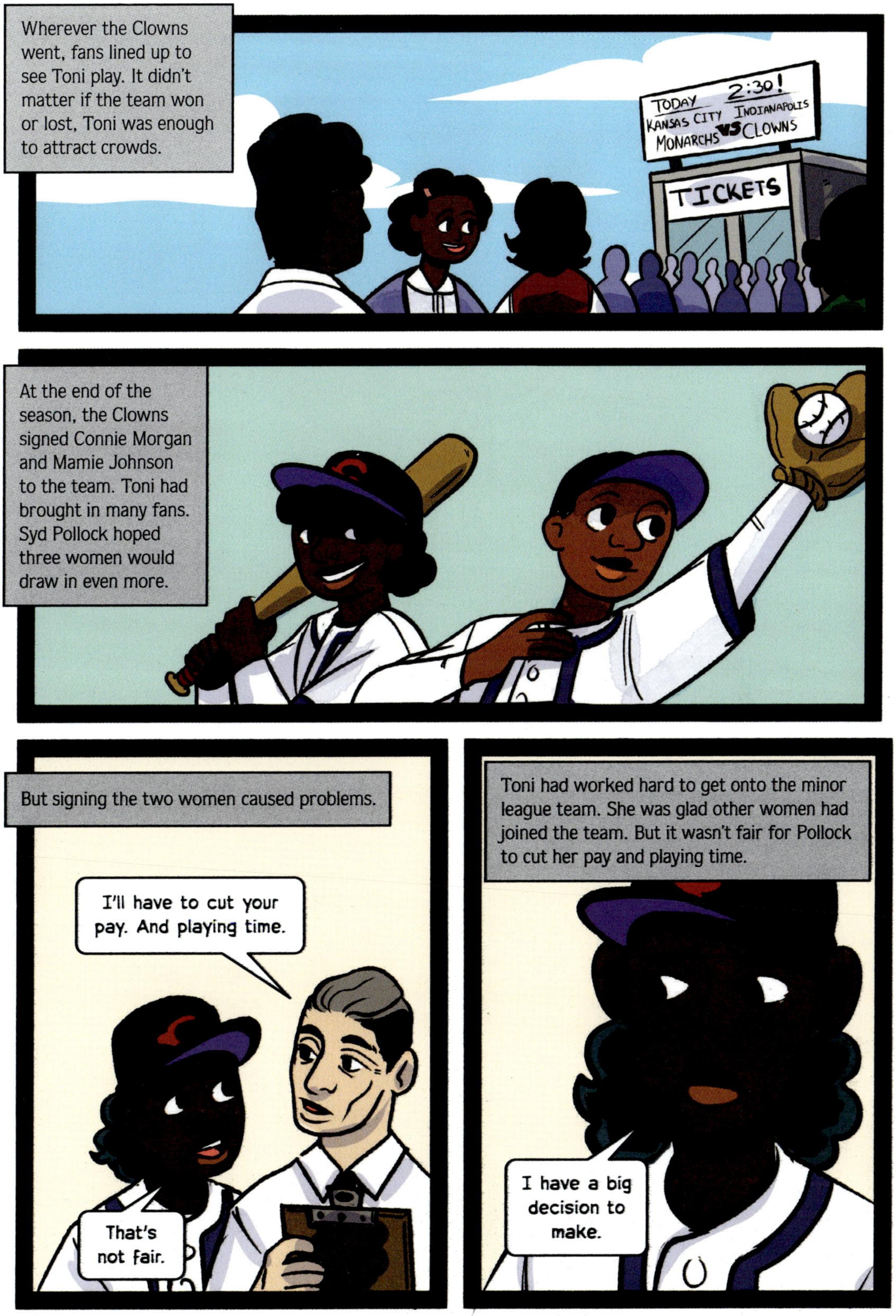
Wherever the Clowns went, fans lined up to see Toni play. It didn't matter if the team won or lost, Toni was enough to attract crowds.
TODAY 2:30!
KANSAS CITY MONARCHS VS INDIANAPOLIS CLOWNS
TICKETS
At the end of the season, the Clowns signed Connie Morgan and Mamie Johnson to the team. Toni had brought in many fans. Syd Pollock hoped three women would draw in even more.
But signing the two women caused problems.
I'll have to cut your pay. And playing time.
That's not fair.
Toni had worked hard to get onto the minor league team. She was glad other women had joined the team. But it wasn't fair for Pollock to cut her pay and playing time.
I have a big decision to make.

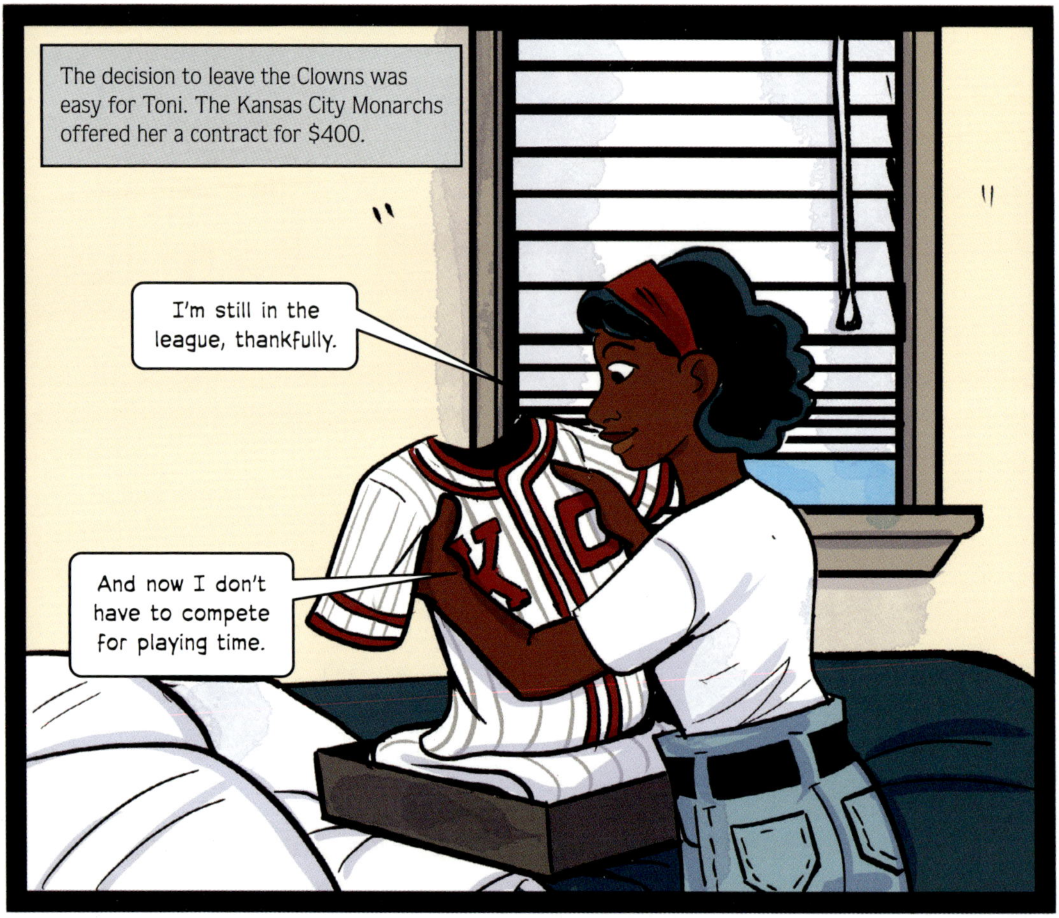

The decision to leave the Clowns was easy for Toni. The Kansas City Monarchs offered her a contract for $400.
I'm still in the league, thankfully.
And now I don't have to compete for playing time.

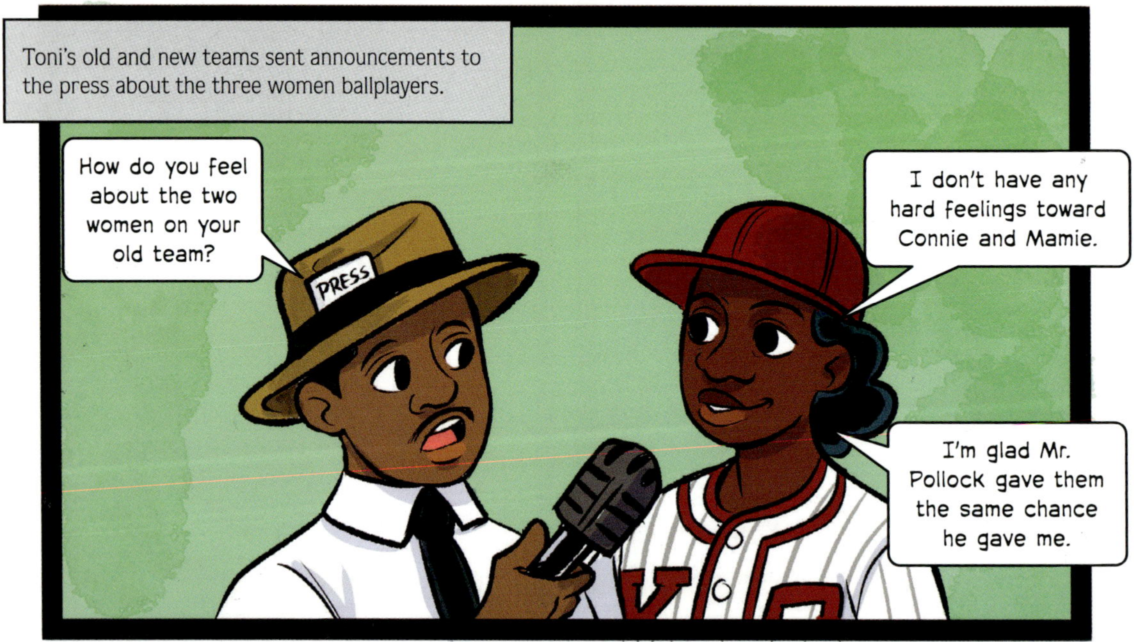

Toni's old and new teams sent announcements to the press about the three women ballplayers.
How do you feel about the two women on your old team?
PRESS
I don't have any hard feelings toward Connie and Mamie.
I'm glad Mr. Pollock gave them the same chance he gave me.

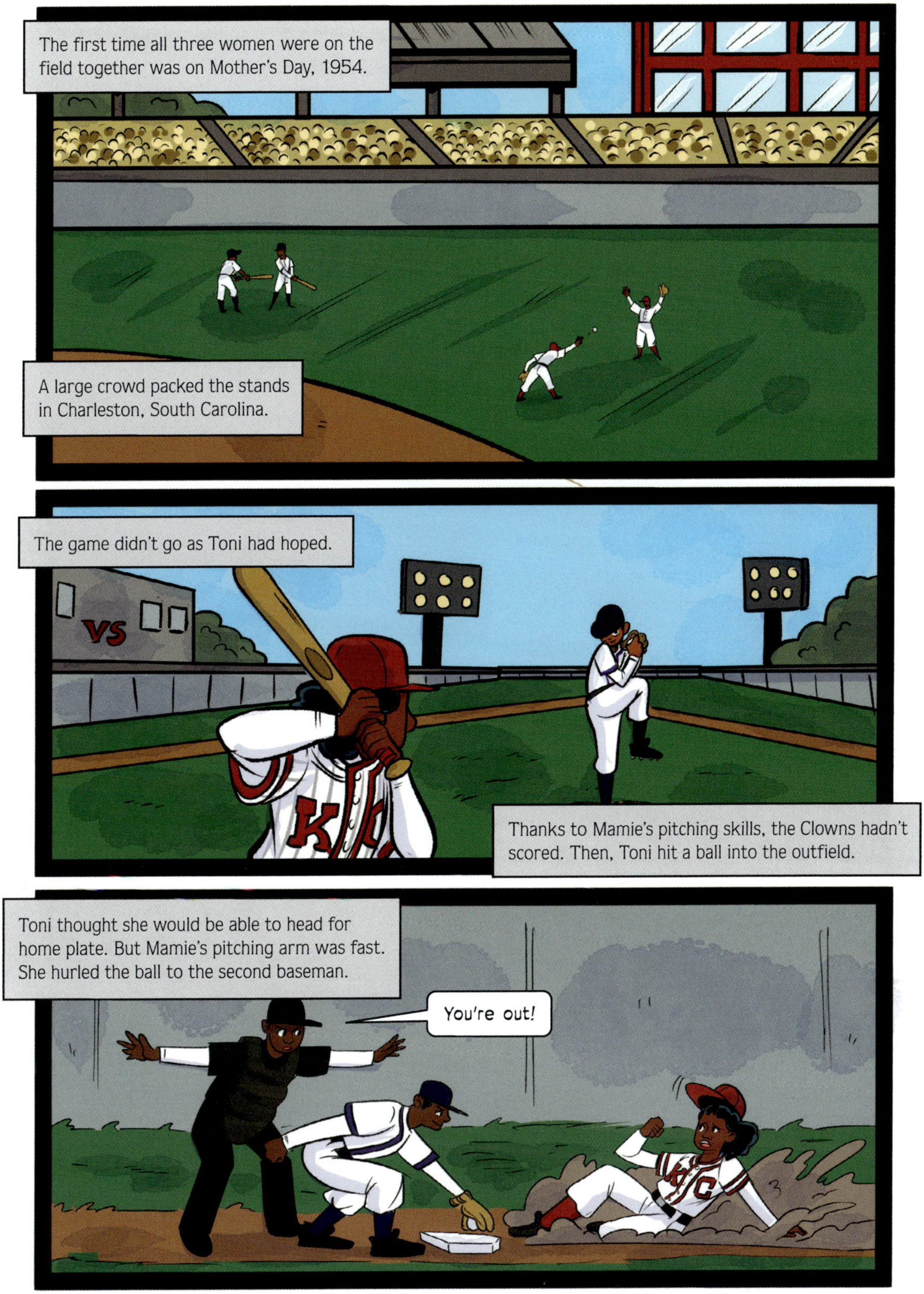
The first time all three women were on the field together was on Mother's Day, 1954.
A large crowd packed the stands in Charleston, South Carolina.
The game didn't go as Toni had hoped.
VS
Thanks to Mamie's pitching skills, the Clowns hadn't scored. Then, Toni hit a ball into the outfield.
Toni thought she would be able to head for home plate. But Mamie's pitching arm was fast. She hurled the ball to the second baseman.
You're out!

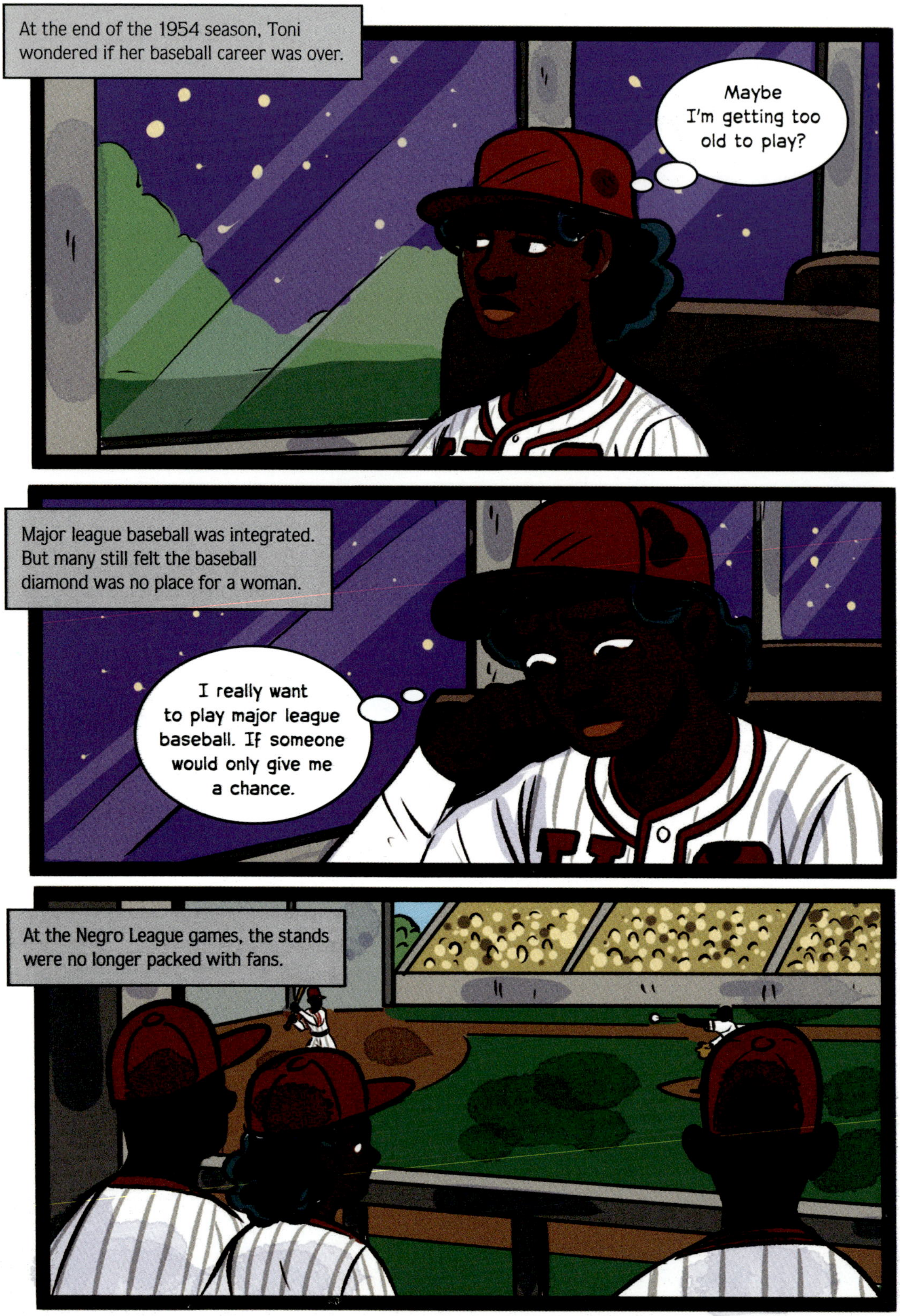
At the end of the 1954 season, Toni wondered if her baseball career was over.
Maybe I'm getting too old to play?
Major league baseball was integrated. But many still felt the baseball diamond was no place for a woman.
I really want to play major league baseball. If someone would only give me a chance.
At the Negro League games, the stands were no longer packed with fans.

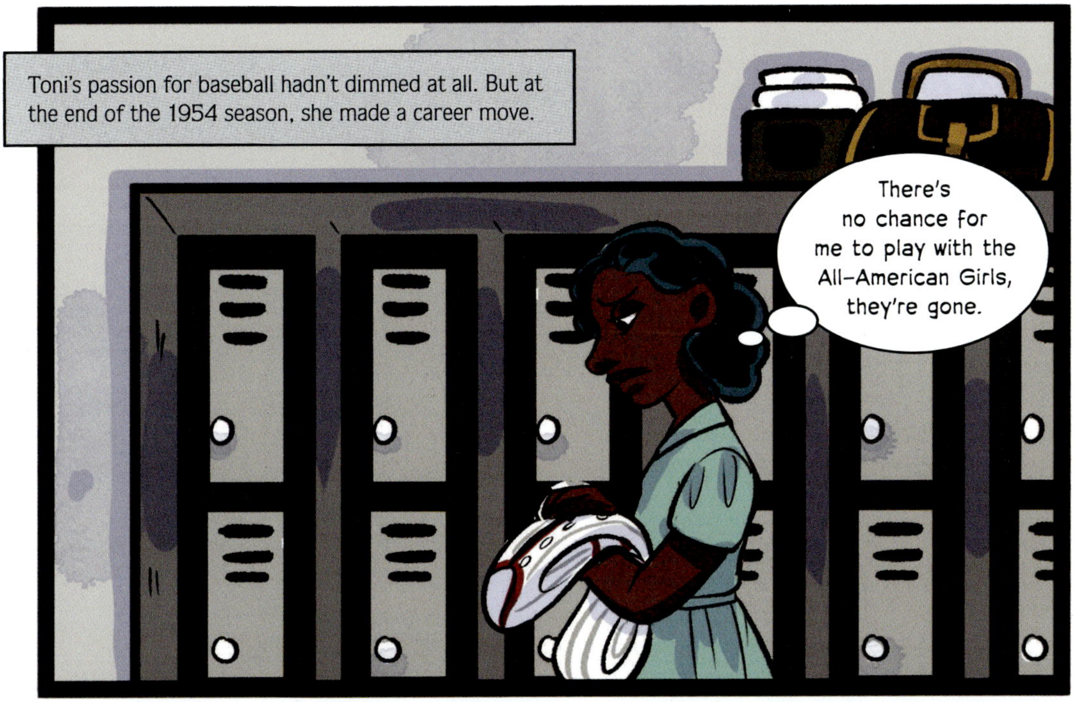
Toni's passion for baseball hadn't dimmed at all. But at the end of the 1954 season, she made a career move.
There's no chance for me to play with the All-American Girls, they're gone.

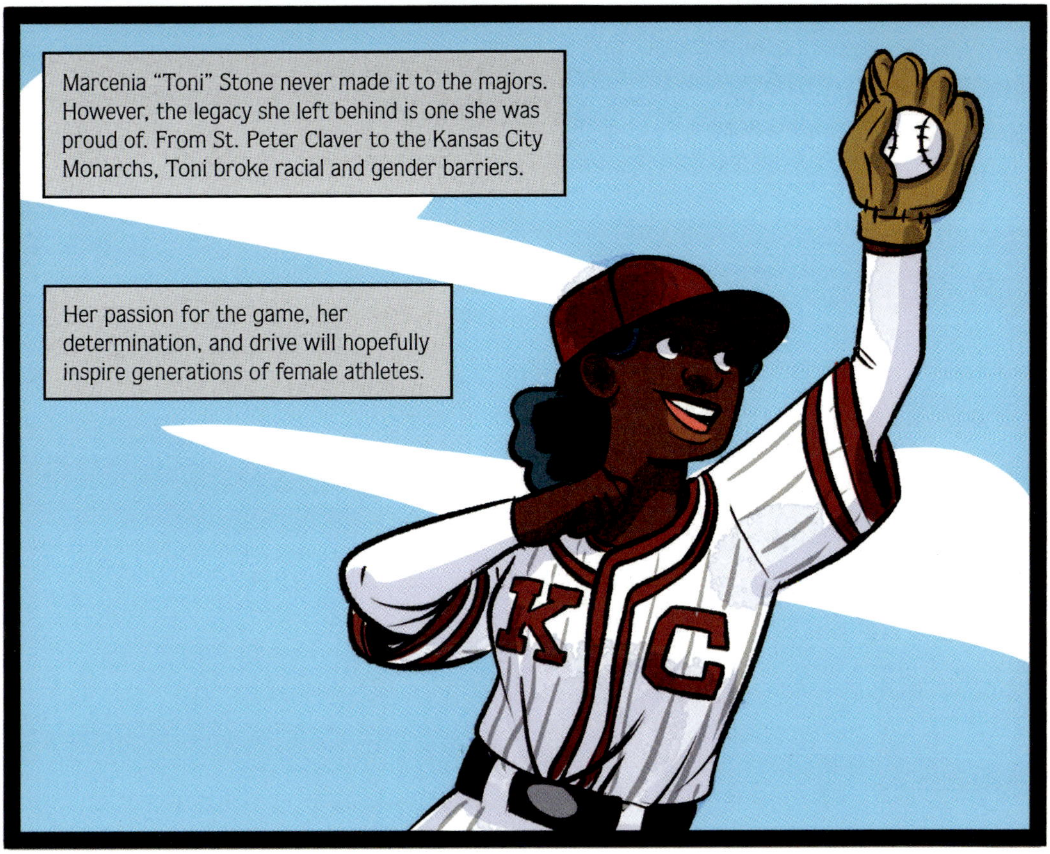
Marcenia "Toni" Stone never made it to the majors. However, the legacy she left behind is one she was proud of. From St. Peter Claver to the Kansas City Monarchs, Toni broke racial and gender barriers.
Her passion for the game, her determination, and drive will hopefully inspire generations of female athletes.
KC

MORE ABOUT
TONI STONE
AND THE NEGRO LEAGUES

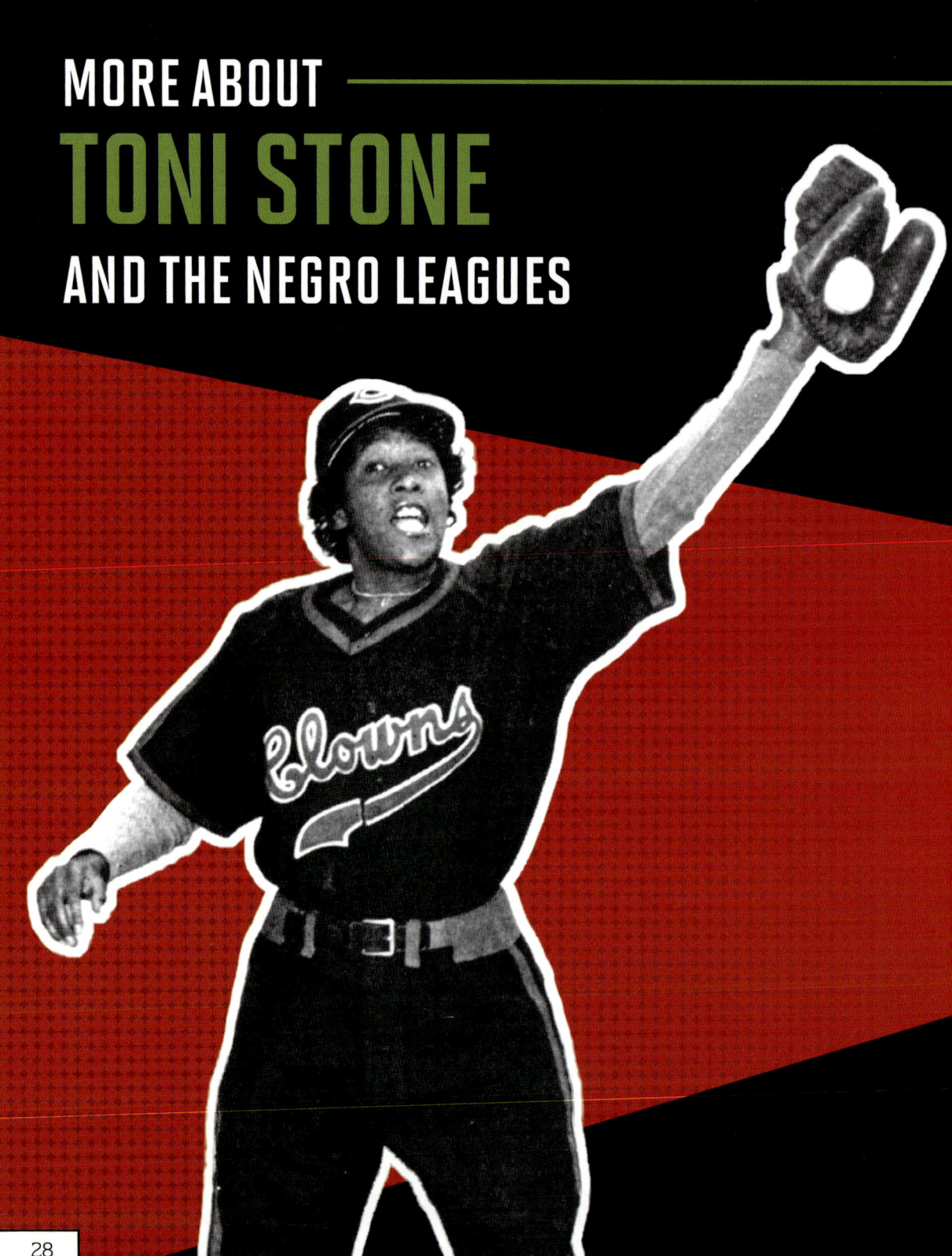

- The Negro National League was formed on February 13, 1920. The last game was played in 1958.

- Major League Baseball's exclusive Hall of Fame has 37 Negro League stars, including legends Satchel Paige and "Smokey" Joe Williams.

- After Toni retired from baseball, she coached several local teams. She also played on a few teams for fun. She officially stopped playing baseball when she was 67 years old.

- After returning to California, Toni worked as a nurse and took care of her sick husband.

- For her contributions to baseball, Toni received several awards. In 1991, she was among 73 players honored by the National Baseball Hall of Fame.

- Toni was inducted into the Women's Sports Hall of Fame in 1993. That same year, she was also inducted into the International Women's Sports Hall of Fame.

- Toni Stone Field in St. Paul, Minnesota, was named in honor of the baseball legend. The field is located in Toni's old neighborhood.

- Toni died November 2, 1996, in Alameda, California. She was 75 years old.

GLOSSARY

athlete (ATH-leet)—someone who plays a sport

barnstorm (BARN-storm)— to travel through the country making brief stops to entertain

career (kuh-REER)—job, especially one requiring special skills or talents

exhibition (ek-suh-BISH-uhn)—in sports, a game that is not part of an official league and is meant to entertain rather than showcase player's skill

insult (IN-sult)—an act or expression showing disrespect or scorn

integrated (IN-ti-grey-id)—no longer separated by race

longshot (LONG-shaht)— a great risk that promises a great reward if successful

racism (RAY-siz-um)—treating people unfairly because of their skin color or background

roster (RAHS-tur)—a list usually of people belonging to some group

segregated (SEG-ri-gey-tid)— to keep separate, especially by according to race

READ MORE

Berglund, Bruce. *Baseball GOATs.* North Mankato, MN: Capstone Press, 2022.

Harris, Duchess. *The Negro Leagues.* Minneapolis: Abdo Publishing, 2020.

Smith, Elliott. *Jackie Robinson Takes the Field.* North Mankato, MN: Capstone Press, 2024.

INTERNET SITES

Britannica Kids: All-American Girls Professional Baseball League
kids.britannica.com/students/article/All-American-Girls-Professional-Baseball-League/309773

Britannica Kids: Negro Leagues
kids.britannica.com/kids/article/Negro-leagues/632672

National Baseball Hall of Fame: Toni Stone, Connie Morgan and Mamie Johnson Blazed a Trail for Women in the Negro Leagues
baseballhall.org/discover/baseball-history/toni-stone-connie-morgan-and-mamie-johnson-blazed-trail-for-women-in-negro-leagues

ABOUT THE AUTHOR

Myra Faye Turner is a poet and children's book author. She lives in New Orleans, Louisiana. She has written for grown-ups but prefers writing for young readers. She has written nearly three dozen books for children and young adults, covering diverse topics like politics, the Apollo moon landing, edible insects, Black history, U.S. history, and science. In addition, she has written over a dozen articles and workbook passages for kids. When not writing, she enjoys learning new facts. Her favorite subjects are interesting lesser-known historical figures, interesting places, and unusual animals.

ABOUT THE ILLUSTRATOR

Markia Jenai was raised in Detroit, Michigan, during rough times but found adventure through art, drawing, and storytelling. Those interests led her to study at the Academy of Art University in San Francisco, California. An avid lover of fantasy settings, cultures, and mythology, Markia has made it her goal to create worlds where people of color are front and center. Diversity within her art means the world to her, and she dreams of the day when everyone will see themselves in media and have the same access to telling their own stories.